Praise

'An authentic and no-frills sometimes-overwhelming wuriq of serviced accommodation. Dave does an excellent job of breaking down the fundamental elements of a successful hospitality business with the potential to reap huge rewards, while leaving the reader in no doubt that this is a tough business in a ruthless industry. I would highly recommend this book to anyone considering serviced accommodation as an option for their property investment.'
— **Katie Jackson**, The Regency

'A great insight into a growing sector in the hospitality/accommodation industry with guidance on how to avoid the costly pitfalls that can arise.'
— **Martin Malseed**, Wealthcare Ireland

SHORT TERM RENTAL REVOLUTION

Maximise your property income using the five-star serviced accommodation formula

DAVE CORDNER

R^ethink

This book is dedicated to my mum, who nurtured my creativity, allowing me to dream; my dad, who gave me the drive and determination to achieve them; my wife, who always supports my dreams, no matter how crazy they are; and my two boys, to whom I want to show that anything in life is possible.

Contents

Introduction

This book is for disruptive property investors who want to take their investment strategy into the twenty-first century. You've been sold the dream by property TV shows and social media gurus. You were promised an empire in six months, 500% return on investment and below-market-value deals around every corner, all with no money down. Now you're in the game, you realise things just aren't that simple. Maybe you have a few properties and you're making money, but not as quickly as you expected. You might have educated yourself and built a solid base and feel it's time to take things to the next level, or perhaps you're just getting started and want to go straight to the highest cash-flowing strategy available: serviced accommodation (SA).

If you're reading this, you know about the turbo-charged income you can make from property when you start renting per night instead of per month. You've seen your property peers making unbelievable claims about the returns they're achieving, but you've also heard the horror stories about 'Airbnbs' being trashed and wonder whether it's something you want to deal with. As with any other property strategy, getting the right education in SA is key. It can either be your most lucrative stream of property income or the biggest liability in your portfolio.

This book will answer every question you have about SA and show you how to avoid the pitfalls. It will also challenge you. You'll need to shift your mindset from tenants to tourists – two very different markets. If you're an investor who prides yourself on doing things the right way, you're in the right place.

I'm Dave Cordner, founder of Central Belfast Apartments, the biggest SA management company in Northern Ireland. At the time of writing, we manage a portfolio of around seventy properties worth over £15 million. I've been involved in SA for over fifteen years (long before Airbnb existed), dealt with tens of thousands of guests and dozens of different properties, and made and learnt from lots of mistakes. I've consistently grown the business and built a brand based on best practice. We've won industry awards, been number one on Tripadvisor for the last three years and are Airbnb Superhosts. We innovate and disrupt, push boundaries to stand out and turn down most properties that are offered to us by potential clients because we know they aren't the right fit for SA.

All the property owners and potential clients I speak to tell me the same things. They aren't getting the returns they anticipated when they started. Their portfolio isn't growing as quickly as they'd hoped. They've lost the buzz they felt when they picked up that first set of keys. They didn't anticipate the hassle that tenants bring and they hate losing money from unpaid rent and void periods. They're disappointed with the direction that legislation is going in. They feel frustrated and impatient, that they're being vilified by the media as rogue landlords living on yachts, when really they've just spent most of the last year's profit on replacing a boiler that packed in.

They know about the unbelievable opportunities from SA but realise they don't have the knowledge needed. It's too much of a gamble to kick out regular income from tenants to chase the dream of making that month's rent in one weekend. They have questions. What if it doesn't work? Is the area popular enough or is it already saturated? How do you start? What are the set-up costs? How do you make sure the place doesn't get wrecked? Most importantly, how much money is it even possible to make?

I get it. You've been in this position before. You might be a bit cynical now you've been around the block a few times with your own properties. You know all that glitters is not gold. This book gives an honest account of not only what is possible but also what is required to make it happen. This is not a passive income strategy – in fact, SA isn't even a property strategy at all – it's a hospitality business that takes serious work, preparation and dedication. But with that comes astonishing rewards.

The book reveals the five fundamentals that are needed to run an SA business, giving you the solid foundations you need to succeed. The five fundamentals will give you the tools you need to systemise and scale your business, to evaluate any property or area objectively, to understand what to expect from guests, and show you how to generate bookings and how to receive the consistent profits you anticipated. This formula will enable you to build a thriving business that you know your guests will love.

SA unlocks the true potential of property by renting per night instead of per month. In Belfast we bring in £40,000+ per year from many of our two-bedroom flats. These same flats would bring in around £850 per month on the rental market. It might seem straightforward at first glance and it's certainly easy to get started – you can sign up to Airbnb in around ten minutes – but it's definitely not an easy business to be successful in. Follow the fundamentals outlined in this book and you'll earn more money from your property and regain your confidence.

Guests are the lifeblood of this business. Deliver for them and you will have the hottest property in town. Get it wrong or don't focus enough on the fundamentals and the whole business will come crashing down. At Central Belfast Apartments, we live by five fundamentals every day. They're reflected in all our five-star reviews. They've led to our business growing with so many beautiful properties and happy clients whom we earn significant returns for on a monthly basis. They have allowed us to survive a global pandemic that decimated hospitality and travel accommodation and they've been honed from my fifteen years' experience in the SA industry. The five fundamentals are:

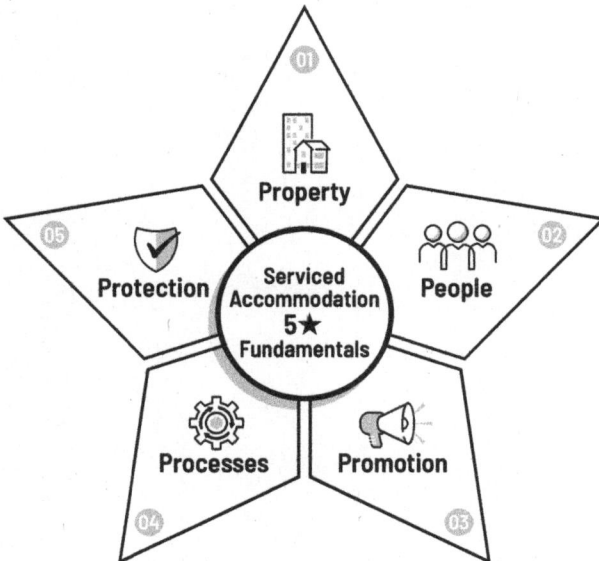

Serviced accommodation 5 Star Fundamentals

1. **Property:** The most critical aspect: how to check a property's viability – what it needs to be guest ready.

2. **People:** What to expect from guests and how to develop the right mindset.

3. **Promotion:** Where to get bookings – it's not just about Airbnb.

4. **Processes:** The systems you need to make your business run like clockwork.

5. **Protection:** How to protect your property from bad guests and not end up a horror story.

1
Get Ready

Serviced accommodation is a fantastic business to be in when it's set up and managed properly. It seriously turbocharges your property's earning potential and can be managed remotely from anywhere in the world. It can be fully systemised and take up only a few hours work per week, while still generating huge profits.

Picture this scene: you're floating on a li-lo in the pool outside a luxury villa in Barcelona, the warm sun on your skin, chilled-out music playing in the background. It's a Tuesday afternoon. Your smartwatch buzzes with a notification: 'New booking: Booking.com. Fri 1st Apr–Mon 4th Apr. £879.' You realise that in this moment, even while you're half-asleep on a li-lo, you're still making money.

You're no longer exchanging your time for money. You have a product that is in high demand and people are paying huge sums of money to come and experience it.

A short time later, it buzzes again: 'New five-star review from John: "Fantastic property, we loved every minute of our stay. 100% will be back."' You smile because you realise you never personally spoke to John – you had someone else communicate with him – but he came and stayed in your property and loved it. He's just let the world know that the high prices they see to book your property are completely worth it. His review is added to the list of all the other five-star reviews your property has. You wonder if you should increase your rates even further, since you have the hottest property in town.

This is what life can be like thanks to SA. This was me last August in Barcelona and is me every day in Belfast, minus the sun and swimming pool. It can be you too. SA is the key to unlocking the life you've dreamt about. Life on your terms. Having a business that runs like clockwork and only requires a few hours per week of your time. You can operate your business from anywhere in the world with just your phone. What would you do if you had time and financial freedom? If you never *had* to do anything but *got* to do whatever you felt like?

One weekend booking in an SA property can surpass a full month's rent if that same property was on a standard tenancy. Remember you have four weekends per month, fifty-two of them every year. You also have Monday to Thursday to sell. The income-generating potential is incredible.

With one property, you could replace your salary. Maybe you love your job and you want to stay in work – well, now you have a lot more pocket money. Maybe you're fed up with your job and the nine-to-five grind – well, now you can leave work and have the same income but all that time back. Maybe you stay in work and save all that SA income – after one year you could get property number two and make twice as much per year, then your income starts compounding and you can scale it exponentially. The possibilities are life changing.

I hope you're excited from reading this. I give you this vision because it is achievable, but throughout this book I will also remind you of what is needed to achieve it. Be under no illusions: this is not a passive income property strategy, especially at the start. It takes significant work and investment to get the five fundamentals set up correctly and running smoothly. It's not easy, but if it was then everyone would be doing it. You will have moments of doubt, fear and overwhelm, but if you follow all the steps in this book you will succeed. This book is a guide to how I have created this life and how you can too.

For those of you reading this book after already taking the plunge and feeling all those negative emotions mentioned above, fear not, this book is for you too. It's not too late. I want to reassure you that with a concerted effort to fix the fundamentals, you too can achieve the business you thought were getting when you first began.

What is serviced accommodation?

There seems to be an endless number of words to describe what this book is about: serviced accommodation (SA), Airbnb, short-term rentals, vacation rentals, self-catering, holiday lets. I want to make it clear at the start that this book relates to each and all of these terms as they are all pretty much the same. Throughout the book, for ease, I will use the abbreviation SA or Airbnb interchangeably.

Effectively what I'm referring to is short-term overnight accommodation where the guest(s) are travelling for leisure or business but the place in which they are staying is not their main home. This term – and this book – applies as much to a boutique treehouse in the forest as a spare room in the suburbs or a luxury city penthouse.

Guests find their accommodation through a variety of booking websites, and they pay per night. The duration of their stay can vary from one night to several months. SA can work almost anywhere in the world, with the specific location influencing the type of guest(s) that require the accommodation. For example, a coastal cottage in a sleepy fishing village will appeal to a certain type of traveller: perhaps families or couples looking for a peaceful, relaxing stay. In industrial or manufacturing areas there may be less of a demand for tourists but a high demand from contractors or engineers being brought in for projects that can take months. In city centre locations, as well as tourists there may be a high demand from multinational companies who are placing technicians or consultants.

What does serviced accommodation entail?

An SA property must be prepared for guests so they can check in and use it as if it were their own. In this regard it should be considered as a large hotel room as opposed to a property that tenants are moving in to. This mindset shift can be a big stumbling block for people coming into SA from a buy-to-let (BTL) background.

Furniture

The property should be fully furnished, including sofas, beds, tables and chairs, and so on. Enough chairs should be provided for the number of guests staying in the property. Furniture should be as high quality as possible – paying guests expect a lot. That said, I wouldn't recommend putting antique or extremely high-value items in an SA as accidents do happen and things get broken. It's important that the furniture provided is durable but also replaceable.

Utilities

All utilities should be fully available to guests during their stay, including electricity, heating and wi-fi. Guests should have full unrestricted control, with the costs of these included in the nightly rate.

All utilities should be set up for direct debit to stop any chance of the balance running out during a guest's stay. Wi-fi should be the fastest available – guests expect to be able to work online from the property and also to stream from services such as Netflix.

The implication of this exceptional brand recognition is that people often think Airbnb would be the only booking site or online travel agency (OTA) any given property could be placed on to generate bookings and business. This is simply not the case. There are dozens of booking platforms that properties can be listed on. Airbnb is certainly a good one, but it's not the only option.

Any property can work as SA

While SA works in an unbelievable array of locations around the world, it's not the case that any given property will be appropriate. As you will learn throughout the book, paying guests have certain expectations. If a property is in a dangerous or unpleasant area, it is unlikely to be suitable for paying guests to stay in. Why would they?

Yet I frequently see property owners snapping up cheap properties, thinking they can get the best return on their investment by renting them out per night. Cutting corners will not work in SA.

It's easy to make money from SA

Property courses and social media gurus might give you the impression that it's easy to make money from SA – that it's just another passive income property strategy. The reality is that SA is not a property strategy at all. It is far from passive income. It's a hospitality business – a small hotel, perhaps with one 'room'. And you're responsible for every job in this hotel: receptionist, housekeeper, security, revenue manager... the list goes on.

SA can certainly be systemised, and you can bring in additional support to make you more 'hands-off' (see Chapter 5). But at the start it's a matter of getting your hands dirty and learning the ropes so you know exactly what and how to systemise things going forward.

Success is driven by occupancy

People talk about occupancy like it's the metric to determine the success of an SA. The reality is it's not much more than a vanity metric. If you come from a BTL background then chances are you have 100% occupancy most months. The only problem is you're not happy with the income or profit. The occupancy means nothing.

The same applies to SA. If someone tells you they have 85% or 90% occupancy, how do you know if they're selling those nights profitably? The goal is to sell nights at a high rate as possible. Rates for any gaps can be adjusted to try to sell them, but you can't create bookings out of thin air. Sometimes nights just go unsold for a variety of reasons.

What are the draws of SA?

There are a number of things that attract travellers away from traditional hotels and into SAs, from cost and convenience of parking to wi-fi and washing machines.

High levels of hotel rooms should not be seen as a threat to SA. Instead, this should be viewed as confirmation that tourism is strong in the area. If people want a hotel, they will book a hotel. If they want an apartment, they will book an apartment. It's rare that one type of accommodation will poach a guest from the other.

Size

Generally, SAs can accommodate larger groups than hotel rooms. Even a one-bedroom apartment with a sofa bed beats two hotel rooms if you're a group of four. Once you go up to a two-bedroom apartment with a sofa bed, you can accommodate groups of up to six – certainly cheaper than three hotel rooms. This represents a big cost saving for groups and families.

But it's not just the cost. Having everyone together under one roof is a big draw for travellers. SAs have living rooms where everyone can chill out together in comfort after a day of exploring – sitting on an actual sofa instead of being perched uncomfortably on a bed in a hotel room. Having separate bedrooms, or even the sofa bed in a different room, gives additional privacy that hotels do not offer.

Kitchens

Cooking facilities are another big draw. Travel is expensive enough as it is. Everyone loves to eat out while travelling, but it's nice to be able to make some toast or a quick snack whenever you like. It's certainly cheaper than ordering room service in a hotel. Parents with young children are able to keep milk cold and heat it when required. There is so much more flexibility with an SA.

Cost

Travellers staying for longer periods will save money by choosing an SA over a hotel. SA operators can offer discounted rates with much more flexibility than hotels can (see Chapter 5). Longer bookings in serviced apartments, even at much lower rates, can still be more profitable than shorter stays because of the reduced changeover costs. For hotels, these kinds of corporate agreements can take a lot of time and work to achieve. Additional savings, such as being able to cook, eat and do laundry in the apartment, are of further benefit for travellers.

Parking

Parking is one of the biggest draws for travellers staying in SAs. Many city centre hotels don't offer it, meaning expensive parking costs at nearby car parks. Most SAs have a parking space as standard and keep the convenience of the city centre location. This is super-attractive to visitors arriving by car and for contractors who may have a work van that they need to keep secure nearby.

Wi-fi

We've all stayed in a hotel where the wi-fi signal is pathetic. It's a frustrating experience, having to sit in the lobby to get enough bars just to send an email. In SAs, guests know they have wi-fi at least as strong as they have at home. They will also have a router they can plug their laptop into if they want a cabled connection. Smart TVs can stream Netflix and other on-demand platforms with ease.

Today, wi-fi is as important to guests as heating and running water. From business travellers to families, they know that SAs offer greater confidence in being able to get online.

What will I have to spend and how much can I make?

For this section I will be using real numbers from the first two properties I ever purchased to show what is achievable from SA. Before we get to the figures, I feel some context is required.

I'm based in Belfast, Northern Ireland – a small city that attracts leisure visitors most of the year round. Nobody comes here for the weather, but the city does get quieter in winter. As a tourist destination, the demand is tiny compared to many other UK and European cities, but it's starting to get the recognition it deserves, and things are gathering momentum.

Because Belfast is a capital city there's a fair amount of business travel that goes on. Lots of regeneration is happening around the city so contractors coming from all over to work in the big building sites. Property prices are also some of the lowest in the UK.

The power of leverage

Back in 2014 I bought my first SA property: a two-bedroom, one-bathroom apartment, about 650 square feet, with parking, located half a mile from Belfast City Hall, in the middle of the city centre. The location of the property was the biggest factor for me – walkable to everywhere with a supermarket and some cafes just two minutes away. We'll talk more about this in Chapter 2.

The condition of the property was quite awful. Two dogs had been living in this first-floor apartment, so there were bad smells and chewed woodwork everywhere. The dogs' owners were smokers, so everything was sticky and brown. It was a true fixer-upper, but this was reflected in the price of £67,500. Back then, the rent achievable on this property was £600 pcm.

Once the purchase completed, I got to work on the renovation. Being my first property, and not flush with cash, I thought it would be a great idea to try to do as much of the work myself to save money. Of course, I did save money, but what I later realised was that because it had taken so much longer with me doing the work, I'd missed out on many potential bookings. A major lesson learnt and one that you will see has influenced me greatly throughout my journey: the power of leverage. That is to use other people's time, money or expertise to get you to your destination or goal more quickly.

All in all, the renovation cost was around £10,000. This included a full new bathroom (tiles, fixtures and fittings), kitchen worktops (I was able to save the kitchen cupboards), kitchen appliances, flooring and repainting throughout and all furniture, including TVs, sofas and beds.

My total investment was 25% deposit (£16,875 + fees) plus the renovation costs of around £30,000. In its first year, this apartment brought in over £30,000 in bookings and it has done so every year since, except during the pandemic.

Spending wisely

As you can imagine, I was blown away by these returns and the following year I decided to buy a second investment property. This one was slightly different: it was even closer to the city centre, about a one-minute walk from Belfast City Hall.

It was a two-bedroom, two-bathroom property on the first floor of an apartment building with secure underground car parking. Apart from the location being better, I knew that having a second bathroom and secure car parking would be a massive draw for this property. It was in a poor condition when I purchased it for £110,000 back in 2015.

Because this property was much more expensive (with a £27,500 deposit) and had two bathrooms and a kitchen that needed to be ripped out and replaced, it cost a little more to renovate (around £15,000 in total), meaning a total investment of around £45,000. I had learnt a lot of lessons from my first renovation about what guests *actually* wanted compared to what I thought they wanted.

I spent my money wisely and put much more effort into making this property look amazing in terms of design and colour. What I created was something completely unique in the market. Straight away it was the hottest property in town and it has continued to be in demand since. It has brought in over £40,000 every year since I opened it. It sleeps six people, thanks to a sofa bed in the living room, and having the second bathroom makes a huge difference in attracting groups of this size.

Our nightly rates range from £150 during the week to £299 at the weekends. These rates are for three-night stays or more. As a company, we don't offer one-night stays, but if we have a weekend one-night gap we sell it for upwards of £400. There is significant money to be made from SA when the five fundamentals are in place.

The rates your property will command will change depending on your specific market, but later in the book I will show you how to do detailed research to identify any property's potential.

How to acquire SA properties

This book is about how to successfully run an SA business. How to source and acquire properties is another book in itself. However, I will say a few words about the different methods you can use to get started or grow. There are three main methods: purchasing, R2SA (rent to serviced accommodation) and management.

Purchasing

Purchasing is the most obvious and straightforward strategy. You buy a property and have full control and ownership over it. Because the income is classed as 'furnished holiday letting' income, you can also claim your mortgage payments as a cost, which is no longer possible with standard tenancies due to Section 24 legislation. Speak to an accountant regarding your situation.

R2SA

The second method is R2SA, where you rent a property from the owner and then run it as serviced accommodation. In this method you have to pay a guaranteed rent to the owner for a period of time. You will then keep the rest of the income, less this rent. There will likely be other responsibilities, such as maintenance, that you will need to commit to.

R2SA can be a quick and cost-effective way to grow your income. You do not need much money to get started and the rent is more than covered by the SA income. All costs are borne by the SA operator. It's a great option for the property owner too, as they know they'll have a guaranteed income with no void periods and also that the property will be well looked after, as the SA host needs it to be in perfect condition for paying guests.

There are some difficulties with this method. Firstly, it can be hard to get past the letting agent gatekeepers who do not want to be cut out of their relationship with the property owner clients. Also, suitable properties may need money spent on them to get them SA-ready. Often properties that are fine for tenants are just not desirable enough for paying guests. Any money spent will improve the quality and value of the property, but the SA operator does not benefit from this as they are not the owner. Should the relationship end unexpectedly, the SA operator will not be able to get this spend back.

Another banana skin is if the SA market gets disrupted, as was the case during the pandemic. R2SA operators were left very exposed when travel evaporated overnight but they still had the fixed liability of rent to pay to the property owners. Even if they filled the properties with tenants, there would still be a considerable squeeze and some sleepless nights.

Management

The third method is management of other people's properties, where the SA operator takes control of a property owner's property and operates as that owner's agent, earning money by taking a commission of the income. In this method, the client (property owner) is technically the owner of the business and the income is theirs. The SA operator's risk is spread much more evenly as there is no guaranteed aspect of the relationship. The client and operator win and lose together.

Maintenance, cleaning and online travel agent commission are the client's liability, so the operator has few costs. This is how I run my business, Central Belfast Apartments, and it has enabled us to scale quickly and survive the pandemic. Having no fixed rents meant we could go into hibernation mode during lockdown and weather the storm. Clients know we are always working hard to fill their properties with the best bookings as we only make money when they do. We have skin in the game and that gives peace of mind to clients who may worry that certain properties are prioritised more than theirs.

Summary

Running a successful SA business gives you the freedom and income to live the life you want. It enables you to work remotely from anywhere in the world, needing only your smartphone.

Your property's earning potential is turbocharged once you start selling it per night instead of per month. SA can work in a wide spectrum of properties and is a perfect accommodation choice for many different kinds of travellers.

SA is very different to renting to tenants. There are a lot more requirements on you as a host than as a landlord and certainly higher levels of investment required at the start. It is not easy or passive income and you can't get away with a substandard property.

The SA industry is still in its infancy and there are huge opportunities ahead of it for those willing to put the work in. SA offers many benefits to guests that they can't find in a hotel or other accommodation. These benefits were highlighted even more during the pandemic but will always be present going forward.

There is significant income to be made from SA and even though the set-up costs are higher than standard BTL properties, the investment is generally fully or almost fully recouped within the first year. The ability to generate the same income from one weekend as a property would from a full month's rent is mind-blowing.

There are several ways to acquire property for SA. Each has their own pros and cons and should be considered carefully before committing. But do not let the decision paralyse you. Taking action and moving forward is the most important thing you can do. Every month you delay, you are missing out on thousands of pounds of bookings.

In the next chapter we delve deeply into Fundamental 1: Property – the most critical aspect of any SA business as it's the only thing that can't be changed once it's up and running. This chapter will give clarity on how to research, select and fit out a property to make it perfect for your guests.

2
Fundamental 1: Property

Having an excellent property is the number one fundamental of SA. You might think that is obvious, but it always shocks me how often people overlook the importance of this. SA is the business and the property is the product you sell.

Without a good product any business is doomed to fail. It needs to be high quality, perfectly in line with the customers' wants and needs and beautifully presented, so the customer feels that they have good value for money.

If a property is highly desirable, this will be reflected in your nightly rates. It will become sought after and will grow a brand of excellence that people will be drawn to. Likewise, if a property is of poor quality and less desirable, it will be cheap and people will steer clear. This applies to all SA properties. It's time to start thinking about your place like a hotel or restaurant.

A strong property is the business's greatest asset. It works for you 24 hours a day, 365 days per year. It's live on booking sites and social media, being viewed by hundreds of people every day. These people are motivated buyers, searching for the right place to come and stay in your area. They have ideas of what they're looking for: price, reviews, quality. They're scrolling through search results of dozens of other places belonging to people who, like you, want this booking. Your goal is to have a property that stops people in their tracks to book *your* place, even though there are so many other options.

Be innovative with your property. Purposely do things differently. Look for a gap in the market and do everything you can to stand out from the crowd. There are lots of different ways to do this, so get creative and have fun.

It's vitally important to get this fundamental right as there's not much you can do to change it. For example, if you decide to buy a one-bedroom apartment then that's what you're stuck with and it better do the job. Yes, you can change the colour on the walls and get a nicer kitchen, but it's still the same property, same location, same size.

Location, location, location

The single most important factor to consider with any property is its location. It's the only thing that can't be changed once the decision is made. Choosing a 'good' location might not be as straightforward as you might think, and you will get immediate and constant feedback from your guests about it in the form of reviews and bookings.

Think like a guest

It's imperative that you try to get into the mind of your guests when deciding on a location. Think like a visitor and imagine what you would want and need during a stay in your place. You might think a property with easy access to the train station is a great location; however, your guests might complain about the noise. You might think a ten-minute bus ride into town is convenient, but your guests might expect to be able to walk into town within five minutes. Right beside a supermarket might be a convenient option, but your guests might complain about early morning deliveries waking them up. Ultimately the market decides if your location is right or not. It will determine the types of guests who book your place and also your nightly rates.

The location of the property plays a key role in the guests' first impressions. Guests arrive at a new place, soaking up everything along the way, constantly evaluating. Picture a family walking to your property, suitcases trundling along behind them. Dad leading the way with Google Maps, counting down the steps. The notification sounds: 'You have reached your destination'. Everyone looks up to see the property. How do they feel? Does mum have a smile or a frown on her face? Does dad feel pride at his choice or guilt for picking the wrong option?

A bad first impression can ruin an entire trip. It can put a negative filter on the whole experience of a property before the guests even step inside. I've heard of guests refusing to even enter a property because they've been so turned off by the location.

Next, picture the first morning after a late check in. Your guest would like to grab a coffee and pick up a few essentials for their stay. They walk outside the front door and try to acclimatise themselves to the area. How does it feel? Is it a short walk to the nearest supermarket? Is it a pleasant walk? Do they pass cafes or parks on the way? Do they see places they want to explore more of during their stay? Does it feel like a welcoming and friendly place? Do they feel safe?

These little things give guests little bursts of dopamine that make them happier during their stay. They give your property extra credibility and value and contribute to better reviews. Guests will mention the great little coffee shop next door or the amazing deli a five-minute walk away.

Remember that a guest's experience is not just based on the four walls of your property. Other businesses in the area also influence how your guest feels about their stay. The amazing thing is you are leveraging these things for free. If you recommend an amazing restaurant nearby, your place gets rewarded for the fantastic meal your guests ate there.

Unfortunately, it works both ways. If the area is covered in litter or graffiti, guests will notice this and mention it in reviews. If there are groups of young people loitering or unsavoury characters hanging about, guests could feel unsafe and unwelcome. Remember that guests are often coming from a

completely different culture to the one they are staying in. They don't know what is normal and what is
risky. Human nature is to default to fear in new situations where things are hard to read.

I've seen properties in my area fail because they
were in a bad location. They were getting reviews
that taxi drivers told guests they weren't safe or
about guests' cars being broken into frequently. If
you read several reviews like that, would you want
to stay there?

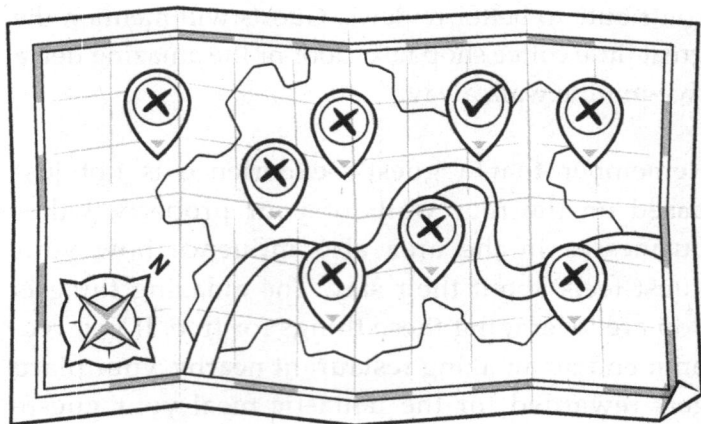

Cheap doesn't always mean cheerful

The cost of a property is a good way to determine its
viability to become an SA. Suitable properties will
not be cheap. They will often be those that property

investors pass over for BTL investments because the numbers don't stack up for that strategy.

Cheap properties in less-desirable areas might bring in a good yield from tenants, but it's a false economy to think they will achieve high incomes as SAs. Reviews will suffer and rates will have to drop. It could actually be the case that there is higher income from tenants than SA once all the business-running costs have been accounted for.

At the other end of the spectrum it gets a little more confusing. The most expensive properties in your town or city might not be the best options either. Often the highest-value properties are larger homes in the suburbs. These are expensive because they are highly desirable places to live for the wealthiest families in the area; there may be prestige from the street name or they may be close to the best schools. But just because a place is highly desirable for people to live doesn't mean it is highly desirable to visit or stay in for a short period of time. Guests don't care about good schools or the best postcode.

Do your homework

How do you work out whether a location fits or not? Ultimately, the market decides and you get your answer from bookings and reviews. However, you most certainly do not want to just cross your fingers and hope for the best. The handy thing about this industry is you can be crafty and leverage the booking sites to learn from people already operating in any area. Once you have found a property you like and think would work, start your due diligence.

Step 1: Look at the map

The first step is to check online to see if there are any other established SAs in the same building, street or area. Open the map functions in both Booking.com (www. booking-map.com) and Airbnb. Zoom in to see if there are any similar properties to yours. It is important that you note whether the properties are, in fact, similar, as if they aren't it will give a false impression for the rest of the steps. (No point looking at information about three-bedroom apartments if yours is a one-bedroom.)

Step 2: Check the calendars

Once you've found some similar properties in your area, open up the listings on Airbnb and check the properties' calendars to see how busy they are. This is a handy way to gauge how popular the area is. Bear in mind that it's not an exact science, as if a host has blocked off nights for any other reason they will appear in the same way as if that property has a booking. It's also not possible to determine what kind of bookings make up the blocked dates – there could be lots of single-night stays or one long booking. That's why it's important to check across multiple listings to see the general trends.

Step 3: Notice the rates

The next step is to check the rates being charged for the property. Look at several dates to get an accurate idea. It's important to check both weekdays and weekends; different lengths of stay, eg one night, two nights, seven nights; and different months of the year. Another method of doing this is to pay for a site like AirDNA (www.airdna.co), which provides a powerful market comparison.

Step 4: Read the reviews

Now you've found some properties in your area, you've noticed what they're charging and seen how busy they are. The next step is to check the property's reviews to see how happy their past guests have been. This is one of the most important steps you can take.

Read as many reviews as you can. What are people saying about the area and about the apartment building? Do they think it's difficult to find parking? Maybe they hate how far away it is from a supermarket. Are there noisy neighbours in the street?

The reviews also help you to see what type of people book the properties in this area. If many of the reviews are from families, you'll know it's a popular area for them. Likewise, you could find lots of reviews from young people or business travellers.

Discovering who the properties in your area are popular with means you can tweak the language you use to market yours. Is it aimed at contractors, corporate or leisure? Each of these groups of guests comes with their own preferences and it is important to discover these so you can be ready and equip the property accordingly.

Step 5: Look at the photos and exceed the standard

All this validation of concept is useless if you don't replicate the standard of the properties you're seeing. Opening an SA in the same street as other successful ones is not a guarantee that yours will perform to the same level.

It's important that you pull out all the stops in a renovation to at least match – but hopefully surpass – the competitors already out there. They have a proven track record of reviews that automatically gives them a head start over you and your new venture. You need to stand out, catch the eye of potential guests and work harder than your competition just so you can get off the ground.

What type of accommodation works best?

When it comes to SA there are a lot of options to choose from. The most common range from the smallest option, serviced rooms; to one-, two-, or three- (or more) bedroom apartments; to houses.

There are also, of course, glamping pods, treehouses, castles, houseboats, etc. I have no experience of these so I won't comment on which type works best. My assumption is that these properties are so unique that many of the rules don't apply. But for the vast majority of SA units it comes down to a choice of rooms or varying sizes of apartments and houses.

Serviced rooms

As the name suggests, guests book one room in a shared property that will have other guests or the property owner staying there at the same time. There will be a shared kitchen in the property or a small kitchenette in the room.

These rooms are popular with solo travellers who may be staying on a business trip or to work in a nearby hospital or university. They can also be popular with cost-conscious travellers who don't have the budget for a whole apartment or hotel room.

Rooms should be thought of by an operator as a hotel room and should have as many amenities as possible to make the stay comfortable for guests. An en suite in the room will give it a massive boost in terms of nightly rates.

My seven-bedroom guesthouse

I own a seven-bedroom guesthouse that used to be a house of multiple occupation (HMO). In the last twelve months, this property has brought in over £135,000 in revenue, with 88% occupancy and an average nightly rate of £58. There are seven times as many guests as one property to deal with, but the income-generating potential is huge.

Apartments v houses

Whether to buy an apartment or a house is a common question I get asked by prospective clients. The answer is pretty straightforward: apartments edge it.

A two-bedroom house and a two-bedroom apartment will have the same occupancy so there will be no higher income from either if all things are equal. In terms of costs, however, there is a difference. Apartments tend to be smaller than houses. That means lower renovation costs, less flooring to lay, less paint to put on the walls, and so on. It also means lower cleaning costs after each booking because it can be done more quickly. Houses often have front and back yards that need to be maintained and grass that needs to be cut. Apartments don't have that issue.

Who takes the bins out and back in if you SA a house? This is a small but significant problem for us and other hosts who offer houses. In an apartment block there is generally a communal bin store area that the building management company maintains. Often apartment blocks have secure underground parking, which is a big plus for guests. Houses in busy locations often have on-street parking.

One factor to be mindful of is that some apartment management companies forbid SA in their buildings. It's important to do your due diligence and check before investing in an apartment building.

How many bedrooms?

This is another common question I get asked and I always give the same answer: the bigger the better. I've touched on it already, but a one-bedroom apartment that sleeps two will have to compete with every hotel room, B&B and guesthouse in the area. If you can fit a sofa bed in, the occupancy increases to four and it's able to attract larger groups.

That being said, a one-bedroom apartment with a sofa bed (that sleeps four) cannot charge the same rates as a two-bedroom apartment (that also sleeps four) because the sofa bed is just not as attractive as that second bedroom. A two-bedroom apartment with a sofa bed can sleep six, but again this isn't as attractive as a three-bedroom property.

Having larger properties means many more group sizes are eligible to stay in the property, therefore it shows up more frequently in searches and has more chances to get booked. For example, a four-bedroom property could either be booked by one person or eight people, whereas a one-bedroom property can only be booked by one or two people.

Larger properties cost more to buy, kit out and clean, but you can charge much higher nightly rates. Our one-bedroom properties tend to average around £30,000 in booking revenue per year. Our two-bedroom apartments do close to £50,000 revenue, but our four- and five- bedroom properties can do £60,000+ revenue.

Once you start accommodating larger groups, you do run the risk of having noise and antisocial behaviour. We'll cover this in more detail in Chapter 6.

What bed layout works best?

Different groups of guests prefer different bed lay-outs. In a one-bedroom property you're always safest going for a double or king-size bed (the bigger the better). But once you go up to a two-bedroom property then what should you do? It really does depend on the type of bookings you think you'll get, based on your research.

If, for example, you think your place will be popular with contractors, they will definitely prefer to have two single beds so they don't have to share. This may be the case for families also, where mum and dad can take the king-size bed and two kids can have their own single beds.

Space is another important decider of what bed layout to go for. Many bedrooms can only accommodate one double with no space for two singles. Likewise, some larger bedrooms can accommodate a double and a single bed, further increasing the occupancy, which should always be your goal.

Getting the property ready

The amenities that you offer play a big part in how often your place gets booked. Booking sites know how important these things are to guests and prominently display what you offer on your listing. These are things guests look for to make their stay more comfortable and convenient. For a detailed checklist of everything you will need to set up your property, scan the QR code at the back of this book.

Kitchen appliances

The more appliances you can fit in the better. People will want to wash their clothes in your place, so a washing machine is essential. A dryer option is great too. Dishwashers are essential – no one wants to do the washing up on holiday and if the guests don't do it, your cleaners will have to waste time washing up once they leave. Remember that you're trying to provide a comfortable, convenient stay for your guests.

Kitchen items

Ensure your kitchen is well stocked with everything guests might want or need to use during their stay. This means, as a minimum, a good set of pots and pans, plenty of cutlery (at least two knives, forks and spoons per guest), plenty of cups and glasses and all the little odds and ends you have in your own kitchen, such as a corkscrew, mixing bowls, sharp knives and chopping boards.

There is nothing more frustrating for guests than going to cook something and they don't have what they need. The good news is that if you've forgotten something, a guest will certainly let you know.

Heating controls

If there's one thing that guests abuse more than anything, it's the heating. If you're reading this book in a warm country, count yourself lucky that you don't have to worry about this – although maybe you'll have air con costs mounting up?

Guests do need to have access to control the heating. But often what happens when it gets too warm is instead of turning the heating off, they just open the windows. A simple-to-use thermostat needs to be installed that will turn off when it reaches a required temperature.

Smart thermostats can also be set up so your (the host's) phone can control the heating. You can set a maximum level and turn it off when you need to. Especially handy if you know guests have checked out and your cleaner won't be there for a few hours.

Bathrooms

We've talked about how adding sofa beds into apartments increases the occupancy. There is another consideration with this: the ratio of guests to bathrooms. Four people staying in a one-bedroom, one-bathroom apartment is completely fine. Six people staying in a two-bedroom, one-bathroom property is a stretch. Imagine the queue for the shower in the morning.

For groups of more than five, I recommend properties with two or more bathrooms. En suites in the master bedroom are a perfect example of this. The more bathrooms, the better.

Seating

This leads on nicely from the bathrooms. It's not a case of squeezing as many people into a property as possible; the property has to be big enough to cope with these groups. If you are sleeping six people in a two-bedroom apartment, there needs to be comfortable seating for six.

Your guests will be spending a lot of time in the apartment and they need to be able to chill out and relax. I regularly see properties that sleep six but only have enough comfortable seating for four or five. This also applies to dining tables: if you want to accept groups of six, they all need to be able to sit around a table and eat together.

People book apartments because they want comfort and to feel like they're in a home away from home. Ignoring this is another example of cutting corners that guests will hate and mention in reviews.

Storage

Guests will be arriving with a packed car or full suitcases. They'll need to unpack and store their clothes and other belongings. You will need to consider how much space will be needed in order for your guests to be comfortable.

Generally, it's less than you think and certainly less than you would have at home. Remember, people are only staying for a short while, so they won't be bringing every item of clothing with them, but also remember that there might be five or six people staying in a two-bedroom apartment, so there needs to be enough.

Sockets

It's important to have enough plug sockets around the property for your guests to use, particularly in the bedrooms. Guests will want to charge their devices, and having sockets by the beds is good practice. It's also important to think about guests getting ready in the morning. Having a socket close to a mirror means people can use a hair dryer or straighteners.

Provide USB sockets throughout so guests from different countries can use their USB charging cables without having to buy adaptor plugs. This small addition will definitely be noticed by your guests.

Parking

Parking is one of the most important amenities to offer. Guests make their booking decisions based on what facilities a property has. If they are driving to your place, or hiring a car when they're there, the number one thing they will look for is parking.

The booking sites bump parking right to the top of their 'filter by' list because they know how essential it is. It is extremely important that you can offer some form of parking on your listing. The gold standard is free, secure parking. Next is off- or on-street parking.

By not offering any parking you will immediately disappear from search results once guests click the box that they require parking. So every single guest that comes to your area with a car will not see your place.

We need to get our properties in front of as many eyeballs as possible to give them the best chance of being booked. If your property doesn't have parking then rent some nearby. The charges are minimal compared to the additional booking revenue that the parking space will bring in for you.

Extras

Providing something cool or quirky for your guests can be the thing that makes people book your place over a competitor's. It can be something small like a coffee machine, free Netflix or an Xbox in the property. These little perks help the guests see the value they're getting by paying for your place. It can also help make the decision when people are stuck with so much choice of properties that all seem similar.

At Central Belfast Apartments we have large chalkboard walls and chalk available for our guests to scribble and create on. I initially thought it would be popular with the kids but actually we've had some amazing artwork created on them. It's also a great way to produce content for your social media channels. Often we have to use Google Translate to make sure what's written in a foreign language is OK to share.

Going up a level, you can offer guests bigger extras like a hot tub, a swimming pool, a balcony or roof terrace, a pool table or airport pickup. Again, you're investing in something that will be paid back multiple times from the bookings that you bring in specifically because of this extra. Just be mindful of the additional work these things will bring, for example a hot tub requires significant maintenance and the water changed between guests.

Wi-fi

Make no mistake, wi-fi is without doubt the biggest and most important facility your property needs to have. It's just an assumption that it's there and it's fast, so you don't get any praise for having it. But if it's unreliable or slow then get ready for an avalanche of bad reviews.

Guests need wi-fi more than they need heat or running water, so make sure you have it set up with a good provider and there's enough bandwidth for all guests to be using it at the same time as well as streaming on the TV or laptop.

Lockable storage

It's important that you have some lockable storage in the property for you and your cleaners, so you can store spare linen, towels, toilet rolls, the hoover, etc. Having everything stored in the property makes it so much easier to service it between guests. And locking it is a good idea, otherwise your guests could help themselves to all your towels and toilet rolls.

Decorating and furnishing your property

This is perhaps where the biggest mindset shift needs to occur in people moving into SA and dealing with guests instead of tenants.

BTL investors know margins are tight when renovating a property. They have to save money wherever possible and know the minimum requirements to get up and running. There can be an attitude of 'that'll do'. Purchasing furniture is more of a box-ticking exercise, eg 'I need a sofa so let's get the cheapest sofa I can find'. The outdated bathroom or kitchen can remain because it's clean and in good condition. That might work for tenants who are paying a cheap rent and don't care about the furniture because they didn't have to buy it. They also view the property before making their decision so there are no nasty surprises when they move in.

In SA the standard of finish required is so much higher. The property is effectively a hotel room that guests are booking for a few nights. Guests are paying customers and expect a lot, no matter what they've paid. They like to feel that they're the first people to ever stay in your property. Furniture and décor must be high quality and attractive. It's not a case of throwing together random pieces of furniture to tick the boxes; there should be thought put into the whole property to ensure it feels welcoming and desirable for the guests.

Bathrooms and kitchens

These are the most expensive areas of a property to upgrade, but the most important too. A tired old kitchen will drag a property down and lead to unhappy guests. So will an outdated bathroom. They don't have to be ultra high-end but they do need to look and feel new and clean. Clean grout between tiles, shiny taps, a good extractor fan and no mouldy silicone anywhere.

Furniture

Again, furniture cannot be mismatched or beat-up old bargains you found somewhere. The furniture in your place needs to feel comfortable and in keeping with the property. If we're talking about sofas, make sure they're comfortable.

An important point is the durability of furniture. Guests won't treat your place as well as they do their own. Wear and tear happen so it's not advisable to have any delicate or flimsy items in your property.

Furniture has to be replaceable as accidents happen. Do not fill your property with antiques or one-off pieces. If a dining chair leg breaks you need to be able to get one more without having to replace the whole set, for example..

Wardrobes

Mirrored wardrobes from IKEA are a great option as they come in different widths and heights to match your room. The mirror on the front not only makes the room appear bigger but it's also handy for guests when they are getting ready in the morning.

Alternatively, you can cut out freestanding wardrobes altogether and go for simple hanging rails instead. These are great when space is tight in your property.

Colour and soft furnishings

Guests will judge a property based on its photos. It should feel warm, inviting and pleasant, not cold and clinical. Spending a little extra on nice cushions, throws and rugs can make a huge difference in how many bookings you get.

Likewise, the paint and/or wallpaper used plays a big part. It is definitely worth speaking to a professional about what colour options and combinations you should make. Paying an interior designer to use their expertise to make your place super-special is a great investment that will pay you back forever.

If you want to design the interior yourself and you've got a good eye, create a Pinterest board and collect ideas of things you like, then put it all together in a way that works for your property. There are lots of different styles you can go for.

I find luxury or quirky styles work best because they are likely to be different or just plain better than all the other properties in your area. We'll talk more about this in Chapter 4, but you want your property to stop people in their tracks when scrolling online. Many properties look the same and if you're offering something unique, you will definitely stand out from the crowd.

Time is money

Another mindset shift from tenants to tourists is the urgency with which you need to get your property online and bookable. In Chapter 1, I talked about the opportunity cost of trying to do all the work yourself: it takes too long and you'll miss out on valuable bookings. It's much smarter to pay the professionals to get things moving fast so you can start taking bookings right away. Plus, the standard that your place needs to be in is much higher than if you were renting it out to tenants, so your DIY skills might just not be good enough.

Budget

It's tricky to give a figure of how much it costs to renovate a property to a good standard as every property is different. On average, a two-bedroom apartment could cost between £15,000–20,000, including a new kitchen, new bathroom, flooring, painting and furniture.

This is a sizeable investment and one that might scare a seasoned BTL investor who's used to a lick of paint and some new carpets, but it's one that will pay for itself so many times over. The desirability of your property is directly related to how much that property will earn. If you don't spend the money to get it to a good standard, you will never maximise the property's earning potential.

Upkeep

Your property will see a lot of use if you've renovated it to a high standard and are attracting lots of bookings. There could be dozens of different guests in it each month. Wear and tear do happen: people scrape walls with their suitcases, sofas and carpets get dirty, batteries need to be replaced in TV remotes and your pots and pans will get worn out. Accidents happen too: guests will break cups and glasses; they'll spill coffee or wine on your sofa. Things will get knocked over and keys will be lost.

There will be ongoing costs to keep your property looking as good as it did before the first guests checked in. It's important to understand that and be prepared for it. The standard has to stay high because if guests arrive and the property doesn't look as it did in your photos, they'll be disappointed and will let you (and all your other potential guests) know in their review.

Summary

The property is the first and most important fundamental required to be successful in Airbnb and location is the most important aspect of it. If you get it right it will be your property's greatest asset, and one you don't need to put any ongoing work into. If you get it wrong, it will be the biggest liability. It's so important to put yourself in your guests' shoes when deciding on a location. How will they experience the property and the area?

Once you've settled on a location, you need to make sure the size and type of property is correct for your market. Doing your research is absolutely vital to ensure you get off on the right foot. This research will give you so many ideas and pointers of what you need to do to get your property set up properly and just who will be booking it.

Once you've acquired the property, the real work begins in getting it ready for guests. There is a lot to think about and a reasonable investment needed to make sure it's fully equipped and highly desirable to potential guests. Again, you need to think about the guests' experience in the property and ensure everything is set up to make it as comfortable and convenient as possible for them.

It can seem like a lot of work but it's a necessary investment and sets the business up for success. It certainly makes the next Fundamental, 'Promotion', much easier. Bookings are the lifeblood of the business and we're going to discover how and where to get them.

3
Fundamental 2: Promotion

Once your property has been acquired and renovated to look super-amazing, it's time to get those bookings rolling in. This is when all your hard work and preparation pays off. You now have a fantastic product, and, like any other business, you need to advertise and sell it.

It's important to get your property all over the internet, in every nook and cranny you can find – booking websites, social media, online directories. You want images, videos, blogs and any other type of content you can use to get eyeballs on your place.

The internet is a big place and there's a lot of noise that you need to cut through to get noticed. If you followed Fundamental 1, you should have a great property so people will listen when you start shouting about it. You need to be smart and remember that the ultimate goal is to get bookings.

Online travel agents

Bookings are the lifeblood of this business. You are always looking for your next one. Unlike a standard BTL where you would acquire tenants maybe once a year at most, in SA you need to sell your property day after day, week after week.

Luckily there are lots of booking sites who want to help you (for a fee, of course). It's important to get your place listed on every booking site you can find. Guests have different preferences of booking sites so if you only list on one or two, you're likely to miss out on a lot of bookings.

Everyone has heard of Airbnb, but you'd be naïve to only list your property here. There are so many other sites that facilitate SA. They are all slightly different, with their own quirks and functionality. Below I've outlined the unique features and downsides of Airbnb, Bookings.com and Expedia from an SA owner's point of view.

In 2022, our booking source from over 4,500 bookings broke down as follows: 57% Booking.com, 21% direct bookings, 7% Airbnb, 6% Expedia Affiliate Network and the rest from Agoda and Vrbo.

Airbnb – 15% commission

Unique aspects

Airbnb is the biggest, most well-known booking site, so you have to get your place on here. Guests get reviewed as well as hosts, and these reviews are visible to other hosts. You can see guests' profile photos (after bookings are accepted). Airbnb also offer insurance.

Listing on Airbnb is straightforward. Once you sign up, you're prompted to enter details about your property, uploading photos and all the information you can. It then gives you pricing suggestions based on similar properties nearby.

In terms of bookings, Airbnb gives some interesting functionality. You can set it up so you only receive enquiries from guests, which you then approve or decline. These enquiries will land in your inbox along with a message from the guest saying they'd like to book your place for the specified dates. You can view the guest's profile and read their past reviews and if you don't like what you read, you can decline the booking.

You can also set it up to accept 'instant bookings' and can set criteria that need to be met, such as guests having submitted a government-approved ID, previous reviews, a profile photo and contact information. This gives a bit more security to hosts that the booking can be trusted.

You can also set up 'Co-Hosts', which gives you the ability to have someone else manage your property and deal with all guest requests. This can be helpful if you are wanting to leverage some of the tasks of the business out.

Airbnb operators who meet certain requirements can achieve 'Superhost' status.[1] Airbnb provide your listing with a Superhost badge and guests can filter search results to show Superhost listings only. These listings arguably give the properties higher standing in guests' eyes and can be trusted more, leading to better bookings.

---

1   Airbnb, 'Superhost: Recognising the best in hospitality', www. airbnb.co.uk/d/superhost, accessed 18 January 2023

Downsides

Because the site is so user-friendly and the most well known, it is completely flooded with listings, making it hard to get noticed as guests have so much choice.

As Airbnb is set up to be easy to use, the functionality it offers is, in my opinion, somewhat restricted. For example, there are only a few cancellation policies you can choose from. You are also forced to only receive payments from Airbnb after the guests pay them, which can make it difficult to collect payments directly from guests for security deposits and so on.

Airbnb are protective of their customers and make it extremely difficult for you to communicate with guests outside of their system. The system hides email addresses and website links in messages if you try to send them to guests.

Booking.com – 15% commission

Unique aspects

Booking.com is an absolute behemoth. It gets millions of visitors from across the world to its site every month. For many people it's the trusted go-to platform for booking their travel accommodation. For these reasons, it's absolutely imperative that your place is listed here.

The opportunities that Booking.com provides for your property are vast. They are a juggernaut of marketing and spend huge amounts of money on digital ads. The vast amount of OTA bookings we receive at Central Belfast Apartments come from Booking.com.

Your place will be shown in search results alongside hotels, meaning that if you have a great property and an attractive listing you can convert people who might not have even been searching for SA.

There are far fewer SA competitors on Booking.com compared to Airbnb. In Belfast there are over two-thirds fewer apartments available to book on Booking.com than Airbnb. This presents a much greater opportunity to be seen and booked.

The functionality that Booking.com offers is incredible. You can choose to take payments yourself or have them do it on your behalf. You can set all kinds of different policies and settings and add loads of information about your property and the area.

You also get complete flexibility around what cancellation policies you want and can have several running in tandem. For example, you can have a thirty-day free cancellation policy but also offer a slightly cheaper non - refundable rate. This flexibility means you are supplying options that suit many more people.

Booking.com also have offices and customer service agents all over the world so it's easy to speak with people on the phone if you have a query or problem. Payments can be collected by the company via 'Payments by Booking.com' or you can opt to be sent guests' card details to take payments yourself.

Downsides

The site only offers instant bookings, which is the main thing that scares traditional Airbnb hosts from using Booking.com. There is no way to receive enquiries like you can on Airbnb; bookings just arrive in your inbox and all you get is some basic info about the guest such as their name and address. In fact, even these settings need to be switched on, as Booking.com want to make the booking process as easy as possible for guests, so by default all you get is a name.

One of the worst and most baffling aspects of Booking.com is that the blurb for your property is generated by an algorithm based on the boxes you tick in the back end. This can result in some strange and frustrating descriptions on your listing. Errors can be corrected by notifying Booking.com, but unfortunately you can't simply write your own description of your property so it's hard to get its essence and unique values to show.

The 'extranet' can be a complicated area to navigate, although they are improving it all the time. Booking.com would have previously only been used by hotels, and the professionals working in those hotels would manage the listings. Now it is populated by more lay people and their SAs, so they've had to make it more user-friendly.

Because Booking.com don't verify the people who use their platform, it can be a hotbed for dodgy bookings and unpleasant guests. We'll touch on this more in Chapter 6, but it is so important that you set your listing up to protect yourself and then stay alert to every booking that comes in.

Expedia - 15% commission

Unique aspects

Expedia is another massive platform to list on. They claim to have over 60 million visitors per month across all their affiliate network and they advertise heavily across all media platforms. Expedia acts as an umbrella for many other OTAs; listing your property once means it will get exposure across many different sites at the same time, including Hotels.com, Wotif, Travelocity, Cheap Tickets, Orbitz, Trivago, Ebookers, Ryanair Rooms, and more.

Expedia has much of the same functionality as Booking.com and is an established rival who also started out as a hotel booking website. There is a lot of flexibility around policies and pricing.

Payments can be taken by 'Expedia Collect' or you can ask that payment details are sent to you to collect the payment via 'Hotel Collect'.

Downsides

It's difficult to get to speak to anyone at Expedia in customer services when inevitable issues crop up with bookings or listings.

Having your property created on so many different booking sites from one master listing on Expedia is handy. However, things do get lost in translation and on some of the more obscure OTAs under Expedia's umbrella there can be some glaring errors that are hard to rectify. In one of our listings for Central Belfast Apartments, the pin on the map was in the wrong location by over five miles!

The back end of Expedia, Partner Central, is much more difficult to use than Booking.com's Extranet and Airbnb's host dashboard. In some cases, if you use a third party to manage your Expedia connection, you may not get a login at all.

Managing OTA bookings

Using OTAs can be a great way to bring in those bookings but they're not always as straightforward as they may seem. From getting paid to avoiding double bookings, it pays to be on top of your OTA bookings and using a channel manager can be a useful way of doing just that.

Payment processing

I've already touched on the different ways of getting paid by OTAs. Airbnb only has one option: they take payment from the guest then pay out to us hosts a few days after they check in. They deduct their commission first then pay out via PayPal or straight into your bank account. This is the same with 'Payments by Booking.com' and 'Expedia Collect', although both of these pay out once per month and in arrears, meaning you could be waiting a while for your income to hit your bank account.

Getting paid this way definitely has some benefits. You don't have the stress of chasing guests for payment as the OTAs do this on your behalf – they move quickly when their commission is at risk! They will also cancel bookings that don't pay on time.

But there are definite downsides of the OTA holding your income. You are not fully in control. For example, if Airbnb decides your guest is due a refund, they will go ahead and process it and you can't stop them. On 'Payments by Booking.com', you still have to pay processing fees to have the booking income paid into your account.

A big drawback is that you have no way to process security deposits. We'll go into the need for security deposits more in Chapter 6, but rest assured you will often feel the need to process a security deposit when you're running an SA and the OTAs offer no support with this.

Another downside is that you are tied to the OTAs for all your bookings, unless you collect payment in cash or ask a guest to transfer the booking income into your account. Cash payments can be tricky as foreign guests don't always have that much cash, especially nowadays. Bank transfers can incur large currency conversion fees and poor exchange rates.

Setting up your own payment processing facility is a must. You can get set up easily with Stripe or PayPal and process booking income from guests' credit or debit cards. You can send payment links so guests process the payments themselves, which protects you from chargebacks (when the card owner claims they don't recognise the transaction and the bank recalls the income from your account).

PayPal and Stripe are super-easy to use but they are also among the most expensive processing platforms out there. If you shop around you will be able to get much cheaper rates, but if you're just getting started then they are a great option.

Avoiding double bookings

Being listed on so many booking sites can seem daunting. The biggest issue you need to watch out for are double bookings. This is when a booking comes through from one site, say Airbnb, but your calendar of availability isn't updated on another site, like Booking.com, to reflect it. The same dates can be booked by a different guest on Booking.com and – boom – you have a double booking.

This can be a tricky situation to deal with and we'll touch on it more later (see Chapter 5), but you don't want it to happen in the first place. There are several ways to stop double bookings from occurring. The first is to only list on one OTA – this is a terrible idea so don't do it! The second is to only list your property on OTAs that allow you to import iCal calendars – a live calendar link that is constantly updated as 'events' (bookings) are created.

Many booking sites allow you to create or export your availability in the form of an iCal link. You then import it to the other sites and vice versa and now all your calendars on your listings are effectively synced up and update each other when bookings come in across those sites. You can also import it into your Google calendar to easily see all the availability.

This method isn't perfect, as there is a bit of a delay in iCal refreshing the new events, so if two bookings across two different sites for the same dates happen around the same time, you could still be caught with a double booking. It also means that you still have to manage your business by logging in and out of multiple OTAs, as your bookings will be spread around them.

Lastly, you will only be able to work with OTAs that allow for iCal functionality, which might be a viable option for you as it's free and does the job reasonably well. The third option is to set up a channel manager.

Using a channel manager

A channel manager is a website or system that you use to keep all your listings on the different OTAs in sync. You can make changes to things like rates or photos on your channel manager then they 'push' these changes out to all the different platforms. This ensures everything is always up to date and consistent, eliminating double bookings.

The benefits of a channel manager are huge if you have multiple properties on multiple listings. It's a one-stop shop for your property where you can see all the bookings and information in one place. It's a fantastic timesaver and we will go into more depth in Chapter 5.

There are many different channel managers available and choosing one will come down to personal preference. In my experience, none are perfect – they each have their own strengths and weaknesses. I'm not going to compare them or mention them all, but some to investigate include Freetobook (https://en.freetobook.com), Zeevou (www.zeevou.com), Guesty (www.guesty.com) and eviivo (www.eviivo.com). We currently use eviivo to manage Central Belfast Apartments.

Direct bookings

It's true that any property should be listed on every bookings site possible to get maximum exposure. It's also true that these booking sites work extremely hard to promote your property and get bookings for you. They are all competing fiercely with each other and will even pay for Google Ads for your company or listing name.

It's tempting to think that booking sites have our best interests at heart. The reality is that they want your property to get bookings so they can earn their commission from you. Airbnb, like Uber, is a completely disruptive business model in the sense that they earn enormous revenues from properties they don't own. They have no loyalty to us as hosts. They use our properties like products that they then sell and they need guests to have a great experience with them so they continue to use the site for all their travel bookings.

For that reason, all booking sites' order of priorities goes like this: themselves first, guests second and hosts last. If there is ever an issue with a booking, they will always look to protect their revenue first. Next, if they can, they will side with the guest to protect their future revenue from that customer. Only if we as hosts have our policies completely watertight and have detailed evidence to prove our case will they come down on our side.

It is imperative that any issues with guests are clearly evidenced and documented and policies are set up correctly on the system. If they aren't, the booking sites will always favour the guests' perspective, even when they are clearly in the wrong. It's a frustrating experience to witness a bad guest play the system at your expense, but it happens all the time.

Relying heavily on OTAs means you are locked in to giving away a minimum of 15% of all your booking income. On top of that, the booking sites exert significant control over your property and your guests. That lack of control over your own business is a common frustration for hosts.

Rejecting or cancelling bookings you're uncomfortable with on these sites can lead to them punishing your listings by making them appear lower down in search results. You may also have to pay to relocate the guests to another property.

Direct bookings give you back control as well as earning you more money. Here are five ways to secure more direct bookings for your property.

Build your own website

If you want to get more direct bookings, it's important to have your own website. First off, it builds trust with guests that your property is actually real. It also gives far more scope to personalise your message and get your brand across than the OTAs give on their websites. The OTAs only offer limited space and functionality to talk about your property and brand.

On your website you can showcase much more of what you're about. There are far more ways to generate additional income by having your own website. You can offer different packages, even giving people the opportunity to purchase vouchers to give as gifts. You can display your social channels and add in reviews from other websites to build credibility. Linking your social channels is a great way to grow a following and being able to showcase your reviews from the likes of Tripadvisor builds even more trust.

You can run Google Ads and Facebook Ads to drive traffic, and if you create blog articles you can get a real boost in SEO. Working on your SEO means that when people are searching for places to stay in your area, your website will show more highly in the search results. Remember, you're competing against the big OTAs, so you need to work hard for those views.

Your direct contact details will be displayed on your website, so guests can contact you before they book to check availability. This offers much more flexibility to deal with enquiries, as guests don't have to search for specific dates like they do on the OTAs.

It's important to have a booking engine on there too so you can take bookings twenty-four hours a day and don't need to reply to every enquiry that comes through. Most channel managers offer a booking engine that can be connected to your website. Some even offer complete website packages that look great and are easy to create.

Offer discounted rates for booking direct

The best way to get bookings on your website is to offer discounted rates compared to the big OTAs. Often guests trust they will be looked after by the OTAs and can be wary about booking with a property direct, especially if the website isn't as slick and polished as the more familiar OTA sites. A cheaper rate is often enough to convince them to book direct. The commission to sites like Airbnb and Booking.com is 15%, so a discount of 5% or 10% is a win for both the host and the guest.

Once you have your own website with your contact details on it, you will start getting contacted by people looking for bespoke solutions for their stay. They may want longer stays, and for these you can negotiate a much cheaper rate per night if you wish. Corporate or contractor bookings can be profitable as there are hugely reduced changeover costs and regular income, so it's definitely worth working to accommodate them where you can. If they can't contact you, the chances are they won't make a booking on the OTA as your property will be too expensive.

Remarket to past guests

Once a guest has stayed and had an enjoyable experience, they are much more likely to book direct for their next stay, even if the first stay wasn't a direct booking. It's important to follow up with guests once they check out to ensure they have your contact details and website.

Again, this is a fantastic opportunity to get repeat bookings from corporate or contractor guests. They may want Monday to Friday for the next four months. Securing the bookings direct after the first visit could save you thousands of pounds in OTA commission.

Keeping past guests up to date with what's happening via Mailchimp (www.mailchimp.com) is a great way to keep your property in their minds for their next trip. You can talk about exciting events happening in your area, special offers you're running or any new properties you're taking on.

Utilise social media

Social media is a great tool to get direct bookings. It's worthwhile having social media profiles for your business and you can keep them updated with offers, photos and other interesting content. You can run competitions and work with influencers to grow your following and build a real community of people who will recommend you or tag you in posts.

Facebook

Facebook is a great platform for sharing photos, videos and written posts. It's a real all-rounder and can be the home of all the different types of content you create. It is great for groups – find ones relevant to your property and get active in them, promoting your property when people ask relevant questions. I'm a member of several groups about Ireland and Northern Ireland. There are constantly people asking for recommendations of places to stay in Belfast and I'm able to share our website. Likewise, there are always people asking about what to do in Belfast or Northern Ireland and I'm able to share my blog articles, which drives traffic to our website.

Facebook is also powerful for Facebook Ads (www.facebook.com/business/ads). For little investment, you can set up ads to drive traffic to your site and generate bookings. You can even upload your email list to Facebook and it will generate a lookalike audience to show your ads to.

Instagram

On Instagram you can use hashtags to get your content showing up in searches for relevant topics to your area or speciality. Because it's a photo-sharing platform, it's perfect for you to share images of your place. We'll talk about the importance of your photos later in this chapter.

Instagram is also now heavily pushing video content in the form of reels. If you can create some cool videos of your property, they have the potential to go viral and be seen by huge numbers of people. Property tours, behind the scenes and cool things to do nearby all make for interesting content.

Because Instagram is owned by Facebook, your Facebook Ads will also be shown on Instagram, and you can connect your accounts so that posting on Instagram will automatically share to Facebook.

Creating Instagram stories is a great way to further build your brand and give a behind the scenes look at what goes on in your life or business. It's a fantastic way to build trust as your audience will watch your journey unfold.

On all of your content you should be directing people to visit your website to learn more or to see your rates and availability. Having people visit your website frequently is a massive SEO boost.

Scheduling tools

If it seems like too much work to manage multiple social media profiles, you can use a scheduling tool like Buffer (www.buffer.com) or Sendible (www.sendible.com), which connects to all your profiles and pushes content out to them all at the same time – a bit like your channel manager for the OTAs. The various social media platforms have different audiences, so it is worth being on them all.

Convert OTA bookings to direct

This one is a little controversial. Converting bookings from OTAs such as Booking.com is a little cheeky (100% not allowed) and the booking sites obviously try their best to stop it happening. They anonymise guests' email addresses, so all email conversations go through their portal, making it difficult to communicate in private. Airbnb and Tripadvisor make it extremely difficult to send contact details via their messaging app because they don't want to be cut out of the process. It's up to you whether you want to use this method.

The importance of professional photos

Amazing photos make a property stand out and help it to get more bookings. Here's the number one tip to get the best photos of your serviced apartment. Are you ready?

Hire a professional. OK, that might not be what you were expecting, but it is the only way. If you're taking photos on your phone or on a mate's 'fancy camera' then you're cutting corners and it will not work. It might look amazing in real life, but if it doesn't look amazing in the online shop window, people will scroll on past.

You need to showcase your property in its best light. Literally, lighting is one of the most important things. Photos that look dark and gloomy are not inviting. A professional will know what equipment is needed to make the place look bright and welcoming. They also know the best angles to shoot from to show everything effectively. It's important that your property looks spacious but also that you don't use tricks or cheats to make a small space look huge – that's just going to be disappointing for guests when they arrive.

With amazing photos your property will stand out in search results on the OTAs. You want to entice someone to choose your property from a pool of dozens of options they're scrolling through. If you have amazing photos, you can even charge a higher nightly rate. People are drawn to shiny, beautiful properties like magpies and they're willing to pay extra for an amazing place. Even if you're in a competitive market and charge a similar nightly rate to your competitors, think about which property will get booked first: the one with professional photos every time.

Having professional photos also subtly conveys to potential guests that this is a professional host that they can be confident in booking with. Having poor-quality photos will make people wonder what else the host is trying to save money on. You've spent all that money getting the place set up perfectly, to make it highly desirable, so it is worth investing that little bit extra to showcase it the way it should be seen.

The only type of photographer to use is one experienced in taking property photographs. They have experience in showcasing the insides of properties for estate agents. Search LinkedIn and business groups and have a look at their past work to see the standard. On the day of the shoot, make sure you dress the property with throws, cushions, flowers, etc. Set the table for dinner and make a pot of coffee for breakfast. Remove bins, fold toilet paper and hide things that don't make the place look like a show home. All these touches help the potential guests imagine themselves in your property. It's aspirational.

The main reason people don't use a professional photographer is the cost. Your photos might set you back anything up to £100 – plus the cost of the flowers and fancy cushions! It's wrong to think of this outlay as a cost, though – it's an investment. After the property itself, it's maybe the best investment you will make for your Airbnb business. These photos will provide a return on investment for as long as your property is operating. All you need is one booking where someone chose your property because of the photos, and they've paid for themselves.

Having amazing photographs also gives you pride in your property. You'll be confident and happy to share them everywhere. They will also provide you with constant content for your social media channels as you will have a portfolio of photos from throughout your property to share.

Summary

You will be surprised at all the weird and wonderful places you pick up bookings from if you put the work in to get your property listed everywhere. At Central Belfast Apartments we get about 10–15% of our bookings from Airbnb – some months it's way less. The rest come from all over the place: other OTAs, social media enquiries, direct bookings made on our website and other general enquiries that come via the website contact details. If you take one tip from this fundamental, it's to not put all your eggs in one (Airbnb) basket.

If you're fully reliant on one OTA you're overexposed, and if it's Airbnb, your property is going to have to work extra hard even to be seen because of the oversaturation that is happening on that platform.

Utilising technology in the form of a channel manager and a card-processing system will take your business to the next level and open you up to many more bookings, as well as ensuring you can take direct bookings. These direct bookings will increase your margin drastically and more than cover the investment in being able to take them.

The next chapter looks at Fundamental 3: People. Once you've got an amazing property and you've plastered it all over the internet, those bookings will start flying in. It will be exciting and also terrifying at the start. Each one of those bookings is a person or group who has just picked your property out of a huge selection of competitors. They will have high hopes.

4
Fundamental 3: People

Once your property is live online, the bookings will start coming in immediately. Most OTAs give new properties a little nudge to get them going, so be prepared for instant traction. Congratulations on all the hard work up to this point. That first booking or enquiry will feel great.

I can still remember mine. I had been a bit bold and set my property live before the renovation work was completely finished, thinking that I might get some bookings for later in the month. But low and behold, a booking came in for the next day. As you can imagine, it was a bit crazy trying to get all the tools out and the place cleaned, ready to welcome the guests. That panic turned to sheer joy when those guests arrived and paid a nice amount for a five-night stay.

'People' is one of the fundamentals required for success because the guests are our business's paying customers. They are the ones buying our products and they all get the chance to leave a public review for the world to see. It is so important to put your guests' needs and wants first in this business. Airbnb is not a property strategy, it's a hospitality business. You are now running a hotel.

Like in any hospitality business, you're going to have to work hard to deliver awesome customer service and get those five-star reviews. Also like in any hospitality business, you're going to have some demanding guests, some horrible guests, some weird guests and of course some lovely guests and, that's right, you need to keep them all happy.

Remember, this is a review-driven industry. Would you eat in a restaurant or stay in a hotel that has terrible reviews? Of course not. And with SA you can be in an even more competitive market than restaurants or hotels, depending on your location. There is no way to cheat and nowhere to hide when it comes to reviews. The only way to get five-star reviews is to offer five-star customer service.

Your reward for offering this great customer service is that you get to charge the highest rates for your property because other guests are willing to pay a premium to experience a great stay. Guests want certainty and if they can see that your previous guests have had a good stay, your place becomes so much more desirable. Social proof is a powerful aspect of human psychology.

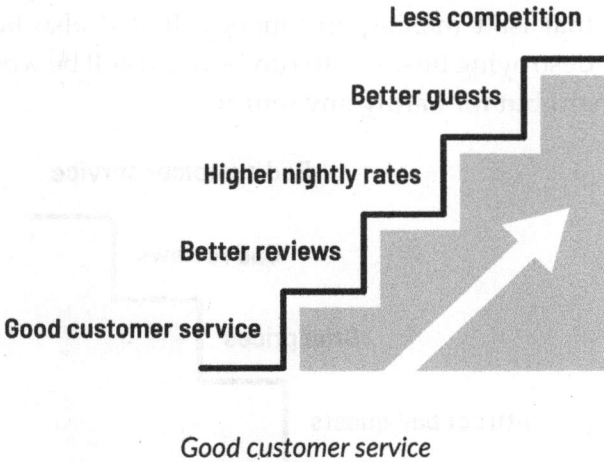

Less competition

Better guests

Higher nightly rates

Better reviews

Good customer service

Good customer service

You also attract better guests to your property – guests who value customer service and are willing to pay that little bit extra for it. By charging those higher rates you weed out less-desirable guests who are just looking for the cheapest option and might not treat your place as you would like.

The opposite is also true. If your place has consistently bad reviews, it's not going to be in demand, and it will struggle to get bookings. People will always opt for a property with better reviews than yours. That means you'll have to start competing on price to try to attract the types of guests who only care about cost – reducing it more and more to always stay the cheapest.

The problem is that other properties in your area with average reviews will notice you dropping your price and will drop theirs too. It becomes a horrible race to the bottom with no winners, resulting in a property that isn't making any money. It will also be a soul-destroying business to run as you'll still be working hard but for hardly any return.

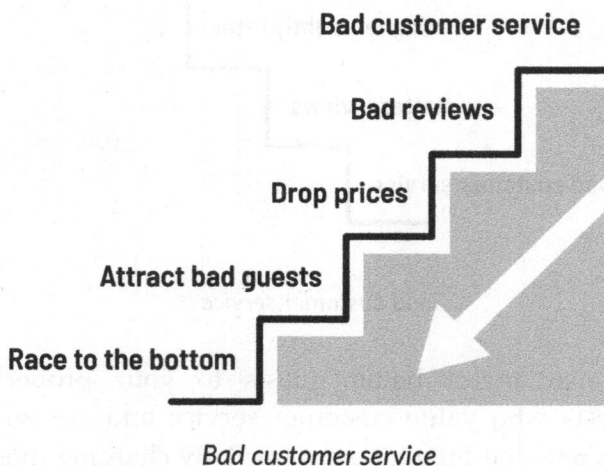

Bad customer service

Bad reviews

Drop prices

Attract bad guests

Race to the bottom

Bad customer service

It's a much more enjoyable business when you're charging the highest rates but delivering exceptional stays for guests and still being rewarded with those perfect reviews. Each one of them is like free advertising. The more you get, the more desirable your place becomes and the less work you'll have to put in to get bookings in the first place.

Picture this: your property is one of 500 in your area. It's also the most expensive, thanks to your amazing reviews. A great booking comes in and you check online to see if this is a busy period with high demand. No, still 499 properties showing as available. Yours has just been booked first because the market deems it the best. This is obviously an oversimplified scenario, but this will happen if you work hard to treat your guests right. You won't be competing with the 500 or so properties in your area; instead, you'll be competing with the dozen or so that are on your level of customer service and quality of reviews. This is a satisfying and secure place to be.

Mindset shift: From tenants to tourists

If you're coming to SA from a traditional property investor background and have some experience of BTL, you will have dealt with tenants before. We touched on the mindset shift that's required in Chapter 2, but it's even more important when it comes to dealing with your customers: your guests.

In traditional BTL, when a tenant leaves, you advertise the property as available. Several people apply and you select a tenant to move in. That tenant will likely be in the property for a minimum or six months but hopefully a lot longer. Your job of filling the property is done.

If the tenant complains about something being faulty, like a leaking tap or a broken washing machine, you'll maybe try to take a look at it yourself or get someone out to have a look at it when they're ready. No rush. In fact, it might take a few reports from a tenant before any action takes place. When you're in the property to look at the leaky tap, you notice the carpet is looking a bit grubby or some wallpaper is peeling. Not to worry, you might think, I'll fix that when they move out or if they complain about it.

The slow pace of BTL is understandable. Margins are tight and tenants are willing to put up with the condition of a property if that's how it looked when they viewed it. You know if you replace that carpet you won't get any additional rent every month, and anyway the tenant hasn't mentioned it.

The difference in this pace compared to SA is night and day. Time is always of the essence and never on your side. Let's look at filling the property. With BTL it's, at worst, once every six months; with SA (as mentioned in Chapter 3) you need to fill your property day after day, week after week, month after month – you're always looking for your next booking. You're constantly advertising it and you have to reply to every enquiry immediately if you want to secure a booking. Guests don't have time to wait around for you to come back to them. They are motivated buyers and there is plenty of choice around. If you don't answer their questions quickly, they'll book with someone else.

When guests are inhouse and report a maintenance issue, you don't have the luxury of waiting a few days before coming out to have a look, then waiting another few days before someone comes to fix the issue. The guests will be long gone by then and will have left having had a bad experience in your place. They will certainly leave a negative review.

When you notice a grubby carpet or peeling wallpaper in your SA property, the threshold for taking action on it is far more urgent than for BTL. Guests have booked your property based on the photos on your listing. If they arrive and the place looks tired and beaten up, they will feel disappointed, which will also result in negative reviews.

Reviews are the lifeblood of your SA business and you're only as good as your last few reviews say you are. If you take your eye off the ball and let things slide in your property, your reviews will also slide. All OTAs average your review scores to give a total, so if you do a great job and have the odd blip it's no big deal. It's a robust metric. In fact, guests will trust reviews much more when there are a few mistakes in there.

But a run of consistently bad or average reviews will drag your overall average down and you'll have to work harder than ever to get it back up. All five of the fundamentals have an impact on your ability to generate glowing reviews, with this one, People, being the most influential. So how exactly can we ensure that guests leave us glowing reviews every time?

The meet and greet

Building rapport with guests is a great way to secure five-star reviews. The best way to build that rapport is by meeting your guests when they arrive. They may have been travelling for hours, they're in unfamiliar surroundings and they might have got a bit lost along the way. Travelling can be stressful and having someone to greet them is a great way to switch off from travelling mode that little bit faster.

By being onsite to meet your guests, you can give the property a final check and make sure it's spotless and ready for them. You can get the heating on if it's cold or open the windows if it's warm. It's also a great opportunity to spend some time in the place checking for any minor maintenance issues that your housekeepers haven't notified you about.

If the guests arrive in a car, you're able to show them the best place to park for your property. If they're wandering around outside, staring at the map on their phone, you can go and get them and show them exactly how to get in.

A warm, friendly smile is a great first impression for your guests' stay – even better if you can help them in with their bags. Once everyone is inside, you can spend some time building that rapport. I would always go through the same process when meeting guests, that way you get more comfortable and confident with each set.

The initial conversation

It is important that you lead the conversation as the host, but it's just as important that you read the people standing in front of you. If they look tired and disinterested or have fed up young children, keep things short and concise. If they seem engaged and have lots of questions, spend as much time as feels right. Always finish on a high note and never overstay your welcome. This is their property now for the duration of their stay

Welcome

A genuine, friendly 'hello' and 'how are you doing?' is a great welcome. Ask them if they found the property OK and how their journey went. I always like to ask if they've been to the area before. If they say yes, you can find out more about when and what they did, what they enjoyed, what they did not have time to do. You can also tell them what has changed. If this is their first time visiting, you can talk about how great a time they're going to have.

Tour of the property

A tour is so important as every property will have little quirks that people aren't used to. If you spend a few minutes explaining these, it makes everything easier and less stressful for the guests and it stops you having to explain it later when the guest can't figure it out. Show them where the wi-fi password is, how to work the TV, how to operate the kitchen appliances, how you recycle, how to lock the front door, where you keep your cleaning supplies, etc.

Recommendations

My favourite aspect of the meet and greet is finding out what the guests have planned for their trip and giving them recommendations based on their plans. Recommendations from a local are so much more powerful than any research they can do online. They are personalised and make the guests feel privileged to be getting almost secret information that other visitors won't get. For example, in Belfast if guests say they want to visit the Giant's Causeway and ask if they should drive or get a bus tour, I can give them information on the best route to drive so they have a great experience or tell them why I feel a certain tour company is the best one.

Tell them where the nearest supermarket is or why it's worth walking an extra five minutes to get to the *best* supermarket. You can let them know about any special events that are happening in the area during their stay or give them a list of cool coffee shops or bars to try. You can mark some points of interest on a map for them and give them your take on the best way to navigate your area, be it bus, Uber or walking.

Any questions?

You want your guests to feel completely taken care of during this conversation. Nothing is too much trouble and you're committed to ensuring they have a fantastic stay. Be prepared for some seriously random questions at this point. It's your job to answer as best you can or tell them you'll find out and let them know asap.

Formalities

Before you wrap up the conversation, it's important to go through your house rules and policies so everyone is aware of what is expected. Things like quiet hours, check-out time and what to do in case of emergency. Go through these and then point them to somewhere in the property where they can see all this information. If you collect payments from your guests in person, this is the time to do it.

Wrapping up

You've hopefully had a fun, engaging conversation where you've ramped up the guests' excitement and enthusiasm about your property and their trip. As you're leaving, say things like 'have a great time at X' or 'let me know what you thought of Y.' My last sentence is always, 'I hope you have an amazing time and, honestly, if there's anything at all you need, please just get in touch.'

The power of human connection

This fifteen-minute exchange is incredibly powerful. They might forget half the stuff you've told them, but they will certainly remember how you made them feel: excited, welcomed, cared for. You've built a positive relationship with them in that short space of time. Your property and you are now one entity in their minds: their experience with you will bleed into their experience of your place, and vice versa.

Even if you never have another interaction with those guests, when it comes to writing a review they will remember that initial conversation. You will see review after review talking about you. They'll say things like 'Five stars! We had such an amazing time in [insert name here]'s property. They were so kind and friendly and gave us lots of helpful suggestions of things to do. Can't wait to come back.'

If you have been genuinely warm and tried your best to give those guests help and suggestions to make their stay the best, they will want to reward you with a five-star review as a way of showing appreciation and saying thank you. This law of reciprocity has been well documented and is a powerful trait in human nature.

The gift that keeps on giving

What happens when something goes wrong and the guests genuinely have a bad experience in your property? Things can and do go wrong in SA and sometimes you can't do anything to avoid it. Say the kitchen floods in the middle of the night, the heating system breaks down or your wi-fi stops working during a stay.

Again and again, I have found that when you have met those guests at check in and built that rapport, one of two things happen. They either give you a five-star review anyway saying something like '[Your name] was such an amazing host and we were having a fantastic time until [insert disaster here] happened. But the host did everything they could to help, and we would certainly come back.' Or if they feel like they can't leave a five-star review, they often just don't leave a review at all. Saving yourself from a bad review can be just as important as getting a five-star review.

Problems with meet and greets

I hope you can now appreciate the benefits of meeting guests on arrival. There are a few downsides, however. For a fifteen-minute conversation, you could be waiting at the property for hours if the guests get delayed and don't contact you. It's obviously necessary that you find out from the guest what time they plan to arrive so you can plan your time around it. Frustratingly, though, guests often don't know what time they'll arrive.

If they plan to take public transport from the airport, for example, they might significantly over- or under-estimate how long it will take to get to your place. Likewise, their flight could be delayed, or they could miss their train and have to get a later one. If guests are driving to your place, they might stop off for lunch or decide to take a more scenic route. They may even be delayed in setting off in the first place.

There are a multitude of reasons why the time they give you can go out of the window. If you are planning on meeting them on arrival, you should keep in contact with them on that day to make sure everything is going to plan, and they know you're waiting for them at the property.

The other problem with meet and greet is that it geographically ties you to your property. SA is a business that can be set up and systemised to run from anywhere in the world. But if you decide to meet every guest, you won't have the freedom that you could have. There are, of course, ways around this. You could pay someone to do this job on your behalf, and family members are a great option. This is actually how I got started in SA – by helping my parents out with their properties while they were on holiday.

Alternatives to meet and greet

Meeting guests on arrival is by far the best method to build that rapport with a great first impression and secure those five-star reviews, but it's not always possible. They could be arriving in the middle of the night; you could have a dentist appointment or any number of reasons. Here are the best of the rest of the ways to build that rapport.

Visit after check in

You can arrange to meet the guests later on the day they check in. This way, you still get to give them a warm welcome, they see your happy face and you can answer all of their questions.

The downsides are you miss the chance to nail that initial first impression, helping them find the place and getting them settled in efficiently. It can also be hard to get a time that works to visit – often, guests pack their schedules with activities, spending minimal time in the property. They might not have time to wait around for you to visit or even understand why you want to come and meet them.

Phone call check in

You can speak to the guests on the phone once they arrive at the property. This way you can direct them to the parking space, talk them through getting access to the property and direct them on a tour of the place.

The problem with this method is that you lose the face-to-face aspect that is so important in building that rapport. And a phone call is only with one person instead of being able to speak with the whole group during the meet and greet.

Remote meet and greet

As we will talk about in the next chapter, and as I've mentioned already several times, SA can and should be systemised to run like clockwork without you needing to be there. Freeing yourself up from being geographically linked to the property is the final piece of the jigsaw, meaning it can generate income while you're anywhere in the world. So how do you substitute that rapport, while keeping those perfect reviews rolling in?

The short answer is you can't. There is no substitute for a face-to-face interaction. When you switch to remote check in, your reviews will dip and your admin workload will increase because you aren't there to answer every tiny little question in one go. But you will be free.

It's important to try to give guests the same information you would give in person, by email, before they arrive. Supplying it in email form means they can refer back to it when they arrive; if you explain everything on the phone, there will be far too much information for them to remember. Emails also give you the opportunity to attach photos and videos showing anything that is hard to describe or more easily understood visually.

The email should be sent before the day of arrival so the guests can review it before they start travelling. The last thing guests want or need is to get a huge email with check-in instructions when they are already stressed out trying to remember boarding passes or driving instructions to a new place.

Good practice is to then phone or email the guests after they have checked in to see how they have settled in, if there is anything they need, or if they have any questions. This should be done even if you have met the guests at check in. It's an opportunity for them to bring up any minor annoyances they've encountered that they might not have necessarily brought to your attention unless you asked for it. It is a great way to show great customer service, turning a minor complaint or question into a great review.

Spending a small amount of time can produce amazing results. Say they ask about the best vegan restaurants nearby. You might wonder (I would) why they haven't asked Google or Tripadvisor, but they decided to ask you. Even if you've never been to a vegan restaurant in your life, you can do five minutes of research and give them a recommendation. If they say, 'Oh, the apartment could do with a potato peeler' or some other random thing, *go and get it*. It's that simple. It's an opportunity to give real value to your guest for free and they will remember that when it comes to leaving a review.

Frequently annoying questions

What exactly do guests ask about? Here's a list of the top things you will be asked. Many can be addressed at a meet and greet. The issue with dropping those and replacing them with detailed emails and guest information folders is that guests often don't bother to read them.

How/where to...?

- How do I get in?
- How do I connect to the wi-fi?
- How do I work the cooker?
- How do I work the TV?
- How do I turn the heating on?

- Where do I park?
- Where does the rubbish go?

Maintenance and cleaning issues

- Light bulbs not working
- TV remote needs batteries
- Door squeaking
- Lost keys
- Smoke alarm beeping
- Anything not clean (oven, pots/pans, toilet, dust found, hair found)

Requests

- Additional keys
- Can you provide (kitchen utensil/extra toilet roll/ extra dishwasher or washing machine tabs/more towels)
- An additional clean

Booking requests

- Early check in
- Late check out

- To leave bags in the apartment after check out
- To leave a car in the parking space after check out
- To bring three cars
- To change dates
- To change the number of guests
- To alter the bed layout
- To send them a left-behind item
- To decorate the property for a special occasion

Recommendations

- Best places to eat
- Best bars
- Nearest supermarket
- Nearest ATM
- Nearest bureau de change
- How to get to [literally anywhere]
- Best taxi company
- Best tour company

This is certainly not an exhaustive list of things guests will want to know. You could answer every single one of the above and still be asked something completely left-field. Every guest's stay is different, and they will certainly throw some curveballs at you. I once had a guest ask me where the nearest strip club was!

Freebies

There are certain freebies that guests expect to be waiting in your property when they arrive. Tea, coffee and milk are a basic hospitality standard throughout the world. Each tea bag or coffee sachet costs just a few pennies. Providing these things alone won't get you any glowing reviews – it's expected. In fact, *not* providing them will probably get you a few bad reviews.

Pleasant surprises

Added extras that your guests don't always expect can earn you some bonus points. Toiletries can be purchased in bulk and replaced or topped up for each new set of guests. Snacks, such as crisps or biscuits, cost a bit more but will definitely go down well and will make a great first impression when weary guests arrive, late at night. Access to a Netflix account on the TV is another little treat – just make sure you don't use your personal account, or you'll lose your place in all your favourite shows.

The most effective freebie? Booze, of course. Alcohol is by far the most effective (and expensive) freebie that you can leave for guests. Wine can be bought in bulk for about £4 per bottle. The price is similar for a six pack of beer. I've lost count of the number of times guests have let out a shriek of delight when I tell them there's a bottle of wine or beers in the fridge for them. It gets mentioned in so many reviews.

If you aren't doing meet and greet, then a handwritten note with their name on it, wishing them a pleasant stay and telling them to enjoy the free welcome pack, is a great personalised way to make them feel special.

Reach for the stars

There's a handier method to get five-star reviews for your property – just ask for one after your guests have checked out. Send them a quick email thanking them for choosing to stay with you and ask them for a review of ten out of ten or five stars. You've got nothing to lose by asking.

I've also found that if you offer guests a discount off a future stay first, they're much more likely to leave a positive review. The law of reciprocity again!

If the guests email back with reasons as to why they can't leave a perfect review, you have valuable feedback to work on for your next guests. You can apologise directly for the failings and express your disappointment that they didn't let you know during their stay so you could have addressed the issue. At this point, you could offer some form of compensation or a further discount. This actually increases the chances that they will refrain from leaving you a bad review. By getting negative feedback directly, you give the guest the chance to get things off their chest and let off steam to *you* instead of publicly in their review.

Summary

How you treat your guests and how they experience your property is what ends up in their reviews. Therefore, Property and People are the two most important influencers of how in-demand your property will be. We spoke in Chapter 2 about what a property needs in order to be desirable, and here we've learnt about the importance of delivering exceptional customer service to guests once they book.

Unfortunately, there's no 100% guaranteed formula to securing five-star reviews. It's not a case of:

Netflix + two bathrooms + free bottle of wine + meet and greet = five-star review

I wish it was that straightforward. Your guests are human beings and they don't work on a checklist; they work on emotion. When they're prompted to leave that review, they'll try to remember how they felt during their stay. Did they feel special, looked after, lucky to have found such an amazing property? They might mention specific things like you, the fancy, free wine or the great coffee shop next door, but it's how they experienced those things emotionally that determines their score at the end.

At the end of Fundamental 3, you'll now have a firm grasp of what guests expect from you. The front end of your business is ready, and you will have happy guests willing to pay lots of money to stay in your amazing property – and to tell the world they're glad they did.

Next, we move on to the back end, Fundamental 4: Processes: the systems that actually run the business. Like a duck on a pond, things can appear calm above the water, but the legs are kicking frantically underneath to keep things moving forward in the right direction.

5
Fundamental 4: Processes

Where you are on your SA journey when you read this book might lead you to have different reactions to starting this chapter. If you're reading this book as research before you start your SA business, you might be thinking that you know everything by this point. You know which property to choose and how to decorate it to make it highly desirable. You know how and where to get bookings to fill it and how to treat the guests that come to stay so you'll generate consistent five-star reviews. If you've already got started in SA, however, you'll know this is possibly the most important fundamental of them all.

Once you get the first three fundamentals set up, things are going to get crazy – very quickly! There are a lot of moving parts in SA and at times it can feel like spinning plates, not giving enough attention to any of them so you never feel fully in control. Your phone will be ringing and your email pinging constantly, day and night, and you'll feel compelled to check, respond and answer everything.

Remember when I said you now run a hotel and work every job in it? Well, this fundamental will help you to identify all the little jobs you now have and show you how to systemise and streamline them to ensure this business doesn't take over your life.

Please do not underestimate how important this chapter is. If you run this business without systems and without leveraging other people, you will become seriously overworked, stressed and burnt out. You'll grow to hate the business and become cynical. Your friends and family will worry about you and ask if it's all worth it. Your holidays, family events and date nights will be constantly interrupted by fires you feel you need to put out. You'll be working so many hours *in* the business that if you work out your hourly rate, you'll realise you'd be better off working in McDonald's.

I know this because I've been there, and I think everyone involved in SA can relate. It can creep up on you slowly, but before you know it you've got anxiety about checking your phone and emails first thing in the morning in case you missed something important, or you'll start imagining you can feel your phone buzzing in your pocket, even when it isn't.

Developing efficient and effective processes is the only way to free yourself up to work *on* the business instead of *in* it. Systems of repeatable, consistent and – where possible – automated steps ensure you can free up more mental real estate to focus on other things. You are leveraging technology and people to make things more efficient and effective.

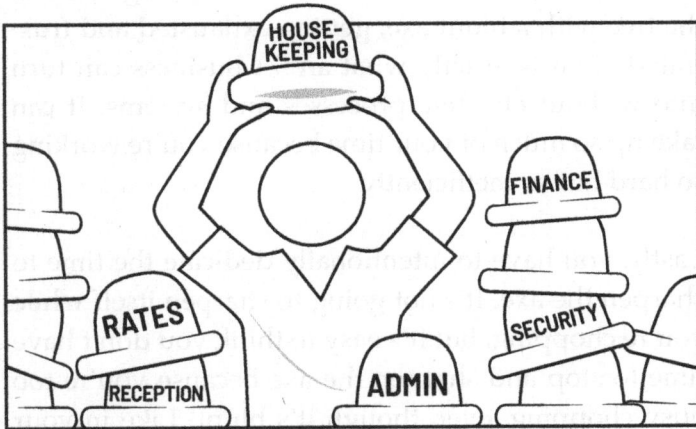

The importance of leverage

The problem I often see is that many people don't dedicate enough time to Fundamental 4. They don't feel like they have the time because they're too busy running the business.

Abraham Lincoln said, 'Give me six hours to chop down a tree and I will spend the first four sharpening the axe.'[2] This is such a powerful analogy in regard to SA for several reasons.

Firstly, it shows the need for leverage to achieve a goal. You can't push a tree over using your own strength; you need tools to help you. In SA this is technology, systems and people.

Secondly, the axe has to be sharp to be effective. Many people would spend the six hours chopping away at the tree with a blunt axe, getting exhausted and frustrated. That is exactly what an SA business can turn into without effective processes and systems. It can take up so much of your time because you're working so hard but so inefficiently.

Lastly, you have to intentionally dedicate the time to sharpen the axe. It's not going to sharpen itself while you're chopping, but it's easy to think you don't have time to stop and sharpen the axe because you're too busy chopping, even though it's blunt! Like in your SA business, things can be so crazy that any time you set aside to work on a system can be easily swallowed up by an emergency or important email, and

---

2   Foussard, J, '"Give me six hours to chop down a tree and I will spend the first four sharpening the axe.": A quote by Abraham Lincoln analysed by Julien Foussard', www.julien-foussard.com/ en/2020/01/29/julien-froussard-abraham-lincoln, accessed 17 January 2023

therefore it doesn't get the attention it needs and nothing changes.

I would recommend stopping to sharpen your axe at regular intervals. It's not just about making the axe cut more effectively; by literally stepping back from the job at hand to improve the tool, you're able to see the tree more clearly, sparking even more ideas of how to improve things. Maybe you're chopping in the wrong place and you notice there's a thinner or weaker part of the tree and if you'd chop there, you'd get the desired outcome much more quickly. In your business, once you step back and start designing and implementing systems, you'll often find what you thought was a good idea from the start actually isn't serving you. Or you'll fix one system and instantly see a crack appearing in another that you thought was already sorted. This constant growth and evolution means you are always moving forward and improving.

OK, enough about the axe! The key points to take away from this are: you need to leverage in order to achieve your goals, you need to make sure you have effective systems in place so that your time is not wasted, and you need to keep stepping back to evaluate those systems to look for new ways to improve. This will enable you to work *on* the business and not *in* it, freeing you up from all those hotel jobs I talked about earlier and giving you a business that you can run from anywhere in the world, with minimal demands on your time.

The areas you need to systemise can be grouped together into several categories. Some will save you time, some will save you money, while others will cost you money but will reward you with both time and efficiency.

Cleaning and housekeeping

This is without a doubt the first job you should leverage to someone else. It's easy when getting started to think you'll save a few quid by just doing the cleans yourself. You think, 'It's easy enough and only takes a few hours, why would I pay someone to do that?' The reality is that it takes up your time at the expense of other more vital jobs that only *you* can do, such as responding to enquiries, answering guest messages and marketing your property.

The housekeeping is a functional duty, meaning many people can do it for a reasonably low rate of pay. The other tasks I just mentioned are much higher value and can be done by far fewer people – probably only you at the start of your journey. Those tasks should be focused on and given ample time.

To give an example, a standard clean of a two bedroom apartment could take two hours and cost £20–30 to pay a cleaner (or you, if you do it). Imagine how many bookings you could secure and how many happy guests you would create if you spent those two hours dealing with these higher value tasks? You could generate thousands of pounds and multiple five-star reviews. Surely that's worth £30?

Cleaning also ties you geographically to the property. You can't go on holiday because you have too many frequent changeovers and need to be there to get them ready before guests check in. What if you get sick, your car breaks down or you have other plans in your diary before a booking appears that means you have to clean?

Even if you're happy to give up the six or more hours per week that it would take you to clean an apartment a few times, it's important to remember that you don't get to decide when those hours are! Bookings come in at random times and changeovers almost always happen on Sundays. You might think it will only take two hours, but you could arrive to find the guests still in bed or evidence of a party that will take all day to get back to normal, ready for the next guests to arrive.

You're also unlikely to grow past one property because you'll be so overworked from doing all the jobs in your first that a second would tip you over the edge. Freeing yourself up from cleaning the properties is the biggest freedom shift you will have in this business and will show you the possibilities of leveraging other tasks out.

Who should clean your property?

There are several options when trying to free yourself from cleaning your property.

A family member

Enlist a young family member, such as a son or daughter, nephew or niece. Younger family members can be keen to earn a few extra pounds and you know you can trust them to show up on time, listen to instructions and do a decent job. This is actually how I started, cleaning for my parents in their first properties.

A cleaning agency

Engaging a cleaning agency to come and look after your property has its pros and cons. The benefits are that they probably have a team of cleaners, which means even if one is sick, another can take their place. All you need to do is send your list to your contact in the agency and they will do all the work in arranging the cleaner. They will supply their own cleaning products, which is another saving to you. Many also claim to specialise in SA cleans.

There are several downsides to this method. Firstly, you are likely to have different cleaners coming to your property on every clean. It takes repetition to get efficient at cleaning a property. You need to become familiar with it and notice which parts need extra attention. Someone new coming in every time means that they are likely to be slower and do a worse job than someone who cleans your place every time.

Secondly, it's a common occurrence that agency cleaners just don't show up to jobs. Your contact in the agency has scheduled the clean but no one knows the cleaner didn't show up until you or your guests arrive. The stress of walking into an uncleaned apartment thirty minutes before guests arrive is something else.

Thirdly, it is the most expensive option. An agency will be paying their cleaners around minimum wage then adding a markup onto the price you pay for themselves. This can make for a frustrating experience when you're paying high prices but getting different cleaners every time – some that don't even show up.

Lastly, if your relationship with the agency ever comes to an abrupt end, for example because they dump you as a client if you're regularly feeding back things that a cleaner has missed, you are in trouble. This has happened to me twice: once when we had around ten apartments and once when we had twenty. Knowing you have twenty cleans in one weekend and no cleaners to do them is a scary thought. By relying on an agency, you are very exposed to this happening. For that reason, I much prefer to employ cleaners individually.

An individual cleaner

By using an individual cleaner (or cleaners) you will have consistency with the same people cleaning the property each time. It's also cheaper than using an agency. You can build a much closer relationship with your cleaning staff, but likewise if they aren't doing a great job they can be replaced, with the others picking up the slack in the meantime.

When trying to source cleaners, it's important to look for people with hotel or housekeeping experience. Remember you are running a hotel and your housekeeping team needs to operate that way; for example, beds need to look perfect every time. You need everything to be left in a certain way and in its place. While hotel housekeepers are trained in this, domestic cleaners often struggle to grasp it. Domestic cleaners will never look in clients' cupboards or drawers, but you will need your housekeepers to check every cupboard and drawer and empty them. The last thing a guest wants to see is the previous guest's dirty underwear left in a drawer or leftover food still in the fridge.

Let me be clear, leveraging out your cleaning is necessary but certainly not easy. It will always be a thorn in your side and is one of the trickiest systems in this business to get right. No one will ever clean your property as well as you can. The cleaning profession is a transitory one, meaning cleaners come and go regularly. Outsourcing cleaning will require dedicating ongoing time to it, but it certainly provides the greatest reward of both time and freedom.

Laundry

After cleaning, the next job to leverage is the hotel laundry room. Your bed linen and towels obviously need to be replaced after each set of guests.

Who should launder the linen and towels?

There is a spectrum here, depending on how leveraged you want to go. At one end of the spectrum, you buy three sets of linen and towels. While one is on the beds, another is in your storage cupboard in the property, ready for the next changeover, and the third is being cleaned.

You need to decide who cleans the linen. I would advise it not to be you for the same reasons as the cleaning. You are tied to the property, and you can't experience freedom if you have to wash and iron every towel and pillowcase that gets used. There are therefore two alternatives.

A laundrette

In this scenario, your cleaner takes the dirty linen to a laundrette who washes, dries and irons it, ready to be picked up after the cleaner drops off the next load of dirty washing. There is obviously a cost to this, but it saves you valuable time and also saves your utility bills from all that laundry.

The downside is that you'll have to also pay your cleaner for their time dropping it to and from the laundrette. Another less obvious problem with this method is that quickly those three sets of linen will become washed out, stained by guests' fake tan or worse. They could become frayed and get ripped and then you'll need to replace them. Big rips or bad stains are an obvious sign they need to be replaced, but often it's a slower deterioration and it can be difficult to decide on the exact moment to replace them.

A professional linen company

The best practice regarding linen is to hire it from a professional hotel bedding provider. You will be given hotel-quality bedding and towels, giving the guests an impression of luxury and hopefully a great night's sleep. Guests will recognise it and mention it in reviews. The linen company does its own quality control and replaces items without you ever having to think about it. They will also deliver clean linen and pick up dirty linen.

The price will certainly be higher than going to the laundrette, but you'll have complete piece of mind knowing you've outsourced a key task to a professional outfit who are dealing with businesses much larger than yours. It's another step towards realising your identity of being a mini hotel.

Maintenance

As previously mentioned, things can and do go wrong in SA – not every stay, but relatively frequently. And when they do it's important to react quickly to address the problem. You need to have a team of tradespeople you can call on in these times. If you can get a good all-round handyman, this will help you too.

Having someone you can call when a guest reports an issue means that you won't ever be needed in person when you aren't available. You are wanting to deliver fast and effective resolutions to guests' complaints and telling them you can't come to the property until, for example, you come back from work isn't ideal.

Using a professional means that when they see the problem, they will know how to fix it quickly and properly. They will have the right tools and experience to make sure the job is done right. At the start of my journey, I used to drop everything and go to the property once a guest reported something amiss. Tool bag in hand, I would quickly realise I had no idea what I was doing and my attempt at a DIY repair would not last long. I would either end up stressed and embarrassed, trying to fix something while the guests watched on in disbelief, or I would see the problem was way out of my skill set and call a professional, meaning I'd wasted my time attempting to fix it in the first place.

The importance of troubleshooting

Once you're outsourcing your maintenance to a professional, it's important that you implement a system for troubleshooting problems with guests before you make the call to the tradesperson. A complaint from the guest that the heating isn't working is not enough information for you to call a gas engineer.

Troubleshooting questions to ask your guests

- Are any of the radiators working?
- Is there hot water?
- Can you look at the boiler and tell me if it's on?
- Are there any fault codes showing?

- Have you set the thermostat to the required temperature?

These questions give you more information and often problems like this can be fixed in a few seconds, which is great for the guest and saves you the call-out fee from a gas engineer who potentially only has to turn the boiler on.

How troubleshooting can save you time, stress and money

Below are just some of the issues that guests have brought to us in the past that with one or two questions we have been able to solve:

- **The wi-fi isn't working:** The guest might be using the admin password for logging on to the router instead of the wi-fi password.

- **The key safe won't open:** The guest might not know how to operate the key safe.

- **The door won't lock:** The guest might not realise they need to lift the handle before turning the key.

- **The car park shutter won't open:** The guest could be pushing the wrong button on the key fob.

The great thing about having these issues brought to our attention is that each one can be documented and put into a guest information folder so you can direct future guests to look at it and see photos of how to use or do these things properly.

Using video for guest advice

Use video for anything that is hard to describe in words. For example, if you have a key safe hidden in a hard-to-find place, shoot a quick video showing exactly where it is located. Send this YouTube link to every guest before check in, encouraging them to watch the video before they arrive so they know exactly where to go.

You can do this for all kinds of things such as how to find the front door, how to use the washing machine, how to operate the heating or which parking space to use. Video gives the ability to clearly demonstrate something to your guests, even if they don't speak your language.

Using a channel manager

We touched on the use of channel managers earlier, but I want to go into more depth about what they can do for you and your business and why they're a fantastic way to save time and stress. Without a channel manager you have to manage each OTA separately.

Most OTAs will have an option to import or export an iCal link so you shouldn't get any double bookings, but that's only one of the things a channel manager controls. For a start, they get you set up on many different OTAs that you probably wouldn't go anywhere near if you had to manage them all yourself. They push your availability out to them all, so everything is completely live and up to date and your property has the potential to be seen by so many more people than if you just listed on Airbnb and Booking.com.

Channel managers show all your bookings from the different sites together in one calendar or diary. This way you can see all the details you need at a glance. If you're using an iCal and managing the OTAs independently, you will need to log in and out of each OTA to see the corresponding bookings from that platform.

Channel managers also save you time by pushing out any content you add in the channel manager to the OTAs. If you get some new photos taken, for example, you just upload them to the channel manager and those photos are automatically pushed out to all your listings across the different OTAs. This is a massive timesaver compared to uploading all your photos manually to every single OTA.

The same goes for any other changes to your content or your rates. Adjusting things once and knowing they will be quickly pushed out to all your different listings is not only super-efficient, but it also reduces the chances of human error. Imagine changing multiple rates for different dates and having to do that on multiple OTAs. It's possible that you make a mistake and offer a 100% discount instead of 10% or change a rate to £1499 instead of £149. Looking at rate matrixes can make you feel like you're looking at the matrix from the movie after a while!

Rates

I hope this is stating the obvious, but your rates should not be fixed. They should be dynamic and adjust both up and down based on a variety of factors. If you keep your rates fixed, you risk leaving money on the table by being too cheap, but also losing out on bookings because they're too expensive.

Deciding on your base rates can be done by researching the area your property is in. Look on the OTAs for properties similar to yours in terms of size and quality. This is where all the hard work you put in getting your property ready pays off. Your property is hopefully as good – if not better – than everything else on the market. It's important that you took the steps earlier to get it looking its best and kitted out with everything a guest would need.

Do some searches for different dates and see what the other properties in the area are selling for. Make sure you do several searches with different requirements and dates to get an accurate picture of how prices in your area adjust in different conditions.

Factors that will affect your rates

The various factors that will have an effect on your rates include:

Size of group

If you have a property that sleeps six people, your default rate should be set to compete with other properties that accommodate six. It's important to realise that your property will still show up in search results for groups of less than six.

A family of four could stumble upon your property and want to book it, but if the price is for six people, it will be too expensive for four. You won't always fill your property with the maximum occupancy. For that reason, it's a great idea to offer a discount for fewer people booking your place, for example £20 per night less than your six-person rate. This makes it more affordable for those groups of four (of which there are far more than groups of six) so your property becomes much more attractive to a wider group of potential bookings.

I would be reluctant to offer too much more of a discount for solo travellers or couples – no more than £30 per night discount from your six-person rate. They are, after all, getting the opportunity to stay in a bigger property that sleeps six, so the price will always be greater than other properties that sleep a maximum of two.

Weekday or weekend bookings

Depending on the location and type of property, it's likely that it could be in higher demand at the weekend compared with during the week. Towns and cities that attract leisure visitors will always be more popular for weekend getaways.

Your weekend prices can be anything from 50% to 100% or more than your weekday rates, but this will become apparent from your research. In some areas it can be hard to sell weekdays. They often get booked by international travellers or by corporate or contractor guests visiting the area for work.

If your calendar starts filling up with weekend bookings months in advance, you are not charging enough. Likewise, if you only have weekend bookings, your weekday rates are too high and need to be reduced.

Seasonality

Depending on location, your property may experience a high, mid and low season, meaning the demand for stays varies throughout the year. Your rates need to reflect this. You will likely achieve much higher rates in the summer than the winter months.

Also school holidays are a time where demand spikes. This can be tough to take, as the rates in winter could be significantly lower than those summer months.

It's important to look at your booking income over the whole year. Don't get too caught up in the dizzying heights of summer or the potential disappointment of winter. Tourism doesn't just switch off in winter – there are still bookings there to be had – but because the demand is lower, visitors have the choice of many more available properties.

You can't expect to achieve summer rates in winter, but if your rates remain competitive and your property is as good as it should be, you will still get booked ahead of the other properties in your area.

Length of stay

The highest nightly rates will always be achieved for one-night bookings, especially at the weekends. This is for a number of reasons. They are the most in-demand length of stay for leisure visitors, but they are also the most expensive for hosts in terms of costs and time.

Seven one-night bookings will bring in a lot of income, but the changeover costs in terms of cleaning, linen, etc, plus the time costs in terms of communicating with seven bookings over the week, is huge. On top of that, one-night stays are notoriously risky in terms of party bookings (more on that in Chapter 6). Because one-night bookings are so risky, not many hosts offer them, meaning those that do can charge a premium for their trouble. For me, the cost, effort and risk are not worth the money; if you decide otherwise, please be careful.

Encouraging longer stays by discounting the nightly rate is a great way to fill your calendar with more profitable bookings. If you have one seven-night stay, you will only have one changeover and one booking to communicate with – this will save you both time and money.

Reducing your nightly rate for those searches means you stay competitive for two- or three-night searches, but the discount kicks in for longer stays. We offer a 10% discount for five-night stays and 15% for seven or more nights. Most OTAs offer this functionality, and if you're choosing a channel manager it's something you should look for them to provide.

Demand

Throughout the year there will be events in your area that will cause demand to spike. In Belfast we have the International Irish Dancing Championships and the Open Golf Tournament every few years. Thousands of visitors flock to the city and literally every single accommodation option becomes full. There are also conferences, festivals, music events and more. All of these spike demand for accommodation in the area and you should increase your rates to capitalise on this.

Your area will be the same, and it's important that you get to know what's coming up so you don't miss out. Guests are savvy and will book accommodation immediately after a popular event is announced – even if it's a year in advance. So you need to be as switched on as they are or your place will get booked before you even know what's happening.

If you operate multiple properties, you have the bonus of being able to spot a trend or surge in book-ings for a specific date and increase your rates before you're fully booked. If you only manage one, unfortu-nately you will get booked at your standard rate and not even realise there's a special event on until your guests tell you.

Even if you realise too late that something big is hap-pening and a booking has come in at a lower rate than you would have wanted, increase the rate on the OTAs for those dates anyway. This doesn't change the rate the booking has paid but means that if they can-cel for whatever reason, the nights will be released at the higher rate, and you won't get caught out again. In periods of super-high demand, it is not surprising to see a cancellation get rebooked by a different guest within an hour.

When should you adjust your rates?

If you're just starting out, there are some principles to keep in mind regarding your rates. Managing rates can be a full-time job in itself and if you want to maximise your income and profit, you'll need to spend time on it. There are some tools out there to help you, which I'll talk about shortly, but for now let's assume you're managing your rates manually.

Early booking discounts

Offering discounted rates for people that plan ahead means you can get the run on your competition and have good business on the books as you enter each month. It's nice to see bookings drop in for six months or more in the future. It makes it far easier to spot little gaps and change rates accordingly, instead of having a big wide-open calendar.

Last-minute discounts

If you're coming up to some empty nights in your property, you might want to offer some last-minute discounts to encourage people to book. How much depends on what else is available in your area and what rates they are asking for.

You have a question to ask yourself: would I rather get a booking at a lower rate than I'd like or risk the property sitting empty for those dates and earning no income? As I mentioned before, if you have lots of gaps that you're having to reduce last minute to sell, you need to take a more general look at your rates as they could be too high. Reducing them slightly overall will earn you more income than having to reduce them drastically last minute and still missing out on bookings.

You should first look at your calendar around two months out to see what demand is like and how many bookings are in. If you're less than 50% occupied, you need to start reducing rates slightly across the board. Within one month, you should be pinpointing gaps and making more changes. Within the fortnight, make your final changes to mop up any remaining nights you have available.

To be clear, making drastic changes two weeks from the empty nights is too short notice. By reducing the rates gradually over time you have more chances of getting booked at a good rate. And there's also less stress and panic over empty nights getting closer and closer.

Reducing minimum stays

You now know about the much higher profitability that can be gained from longer stays compared to shorter ones. Another way to encourage them is to turn off the ability for shorter stays to be booked in your property for dates in the medium-term future.

By only allowing, say, five-night bookings for dates six months or more in the future, you can be in the extremely satisfying position of having a calendar booked with brilliant bookings. As any empty dates get closer, you can drop your minimum stay to four, then three, then two nights. There are many more people who want to come for two or three nights than, say, seven nights. But if your calendar is blocked up by two- and three-night stays throughout the year, there is no chance that you will even show up for a five-or-more-night search.

If you have multiple properties in the same block, this can be mitigated somewhat by moving shorter bookings between properties to free up availability for longer stays. Most channel managers offer this functionality, and the movements happen automatically if the OTAs know you have multiples of the same 'room type'. After all, this is how hotels work: they could have twenty standard rooms, twenty queen rooms, and so on.

Using OTA offers

OTAs like Booking.com and Expedia are always competing to get guests to book with them. To help with this, they are constantly running promotions to give discounts to guests. Who pays for those discounts? The poor hosts, of course!

To sweeten the deal, the OTAs bump up search result rankings to properties who sign up to these discounts, meaning your property appears higher in the listings and potentially has a better chance of getting booked. It will also show up on any dedicated pages for that offer, for example, 'Black Friday' discounts. If you don't sign up, you won't show up.

Offering these discounts can be frustrating, but a good way to look at it is if you're likely to reduce your rates anyway as you get closer to the empty nights, you may as well sign up to the OTA offers and reap the benefits they provide. If you reduce the rates yourself by that much manually, you don't get any of those benefits. A handy way to engage with these offers is to just raise your rates by the corresponding discount amount before you sign up. That way your rates remain as they were, but you also get the boosts provided by signing up.

As a side note, Booking.com offers hosts some further 'opportunities' to sign up to. The Genius loyalty programme rewards guests with different levels of discount on bookings, depending on how frequently they use the site, starting at 10%.[3] This used to be somewhat exclusive and reserved for the regular

---

3   Booking.com, 'Get rewarded for your travels: Genius', www.booking.com/genius.en-gb.html, accessed 16 January 2023

travellers, but recently Booking.com has offered Genius status to anyone who has booked a stay.

Booking.com's 'Preferred Partner Programme' is different.[4] It is only available for certain properties that meet the site's criteria for review score and 'performance score'. Booking.com claim that only 30% of hosts are eligible for it. They also claim it provides more page views and bookings. They do it by giving your listing a thumbs up icon, showing guests that your place can be trusted and is a preferred partner of Booking.com. This costs you an extra 3% in commission.

Rate pricing software

By now, you'll be worrying about the complexity of rates and how long you will be spending on them. The fact is that if you do it manually it can take a lot of time. But the unfortunate reality is that it's likely you may not spend the time required and will instead work on an ad hoc basis – only spending time on reducing rates at the last minute to fill gaps, therefore missing out on all the opportunities to increase rates in periods of high demand. I've been there myself. It's easy to fall into this trap as you see the empty nights in your calendar but don't see the additional income

---

4   Booking.com, 'All you need to know about the Preferred Partner Programme', https://partner.booking.com/en-gb/help/growing-your-business/increase-revenue/all-you-need-know-about-preferred-partner-programme, accessed 16 January 2023

you've missed out on by not increasing your rates on a busy weekend.

Rate pricing software is the ultimate way to free up almost all of your time while actually amending your rates (both up and down) far more regularly than any human ever could – and far more accurately too. There are many different types of software that can do this for you, and it's important that you choose one that connects to your channel manager as they will need to adjust them through it in the background. Some are truly mind-blowing in terms of what they do.

Room Price Genie (www.roompricegenie.com) is the system that I use for my company. In a nutshell, it scrapes data from the OTAs in terms of available rates and properties. It knows what availability you have (and should have) and then adjusts your rates based on this information up to seven times per day. No human could work at this level.

Policies

When you set up rate plans on the OTAs, you need to decide on your booking and cancellation policies. Airbnb offers a variety of policies, but you have to choose one from flexible, moderate, firm or strict.[5] They vary between how soon before check in a guest

5   Airbnb, 'Cancellation policies for your listing', www.airbnb.co.uk/ help/article/475, accessed 18 January 2023

can cancel, how much of a refund they'll get if they do, and how much you'll get paid.

Booking.com and Expedia are much more flexible, and you can set up multiple policies to suit your preferences. Best practice is to set up one non-refundable policy and at least one flexible policy.

Non-refundable is pretty obvious: once the booking is made, if the guest wishes to cancel they don't receive any refund.

Flexible policies can be much more… flexible! For that flexibility you can charge a little more – maybe around 10% extra. You can set policies up to have a free cancellation for a certain period and then the booking becomes non-refundable.

It's important to strike a balance between offering flexibility and getting lots of last-minute cancellations. The last thing you want is a flexible policy where people are cancelling the day before check in, leaving you with empty nights and not enough time to resell them.

Pre-Covid, it was common to have a flexible policy that offered free cancellation up until either thirty or fourteen days before the date of arrival. Most of our bookings were non-refundable, however, as people were certain they were coming and therefore they booked the cheaper non-refundable rate.

During the pandemic everything changed. There was no certainty and even a thirty-day flexible policy was far too long. Bookings were generally being made one or two days before arrival as no one knew what restrictions or lockdowns were going to be imposed. No one wanted to be tied into a non-refundable rate if they physically couldn't travel. For that reason, non-refundable bookings dried up and flexible one-day or same-day cancellations became the norm.

Guest communication

Another big drain on your time can be communicating with guests, before, during and after their stay. This, too, can be automated to some degree.

Automated messages

Most OTAs allow you to set up templates in the communication tabs of their systems. Best practice is to have an automated confirmation message or email sent to guests. In it you can give lots of useful information that guests will need regarding their stay, such as check-in and check-out times, the address of the property, the cancellation policy they booked, the check-in procedure on the day (meet and greet or key safe codes) and any security deposit requirements.

The frustrating thing you will find is that often guests don't bother to read these emails and will just come to you direct, either by email or on the phone. There is a fine line between getting all the information guests need in an email and not ending up with an email so long that they'll take one look at it and decide they don't have the time to trawl through it, looking for the one query they have.

For these instances it's a good idea to have prewritten templates for your property that you can cut and paste in response to guest emails. Remember from the last chapter that the questions that come up are frequently the same or similar.

Even though you've been asked a certain question many times before and you know that you sent the answer in your confirmation email, it's important to answer all queries in a friendly way. Always end the email with a gentle reminder that you have put *all* the information the guest may need in the confirmation email sent at the time of booking.

Check-in instructions

If you aren't meeting your guests on arrival, you'll need a way to let them know the detailed check-in instructions and all-important code to access the property, whether that's a key safe code, a code for an electronic lock or the location of the place to pick up the key. It's also important you tell the guests if you are meeting them so they can keep you updated with any delays and you don't waste your time.

You certainly want the guests to be familiar with the check-in procedure long before they arrive, so they know what to expect before the chaos of packing and travelling begins. But importantly, you don't want to send the code out until twenty-four hours before the date of arrival. The booking may be cancelled or may fail your vetting procedures and for security reasons, unless you change your code after each stay, it puts your inhouse guests at risk if someone else knows the code to gain entry to the property while they are still there.

One issue is that emailing the key safe code twenty-four hours prior to arrival doesn't always work. Guests could be travelling on a long-haul flight and not have access to their emails or wi-fi. You'll also find those same guests who don't read your thorough information emails don't read the email that has their key safe code in it. They'll swear they never got the email or have checked their spam folder and it's definitely not there. This is another frustrating but common occurrence that you have to put your 'customer is always right' hat on for.

A good alternative to this is to use a virtual text message service. This way you can also text the instructions to the guests' phones and crucially get a 'delivered' notification, so you know for sure they have received it. This removes the need for them to check their emails. In the text you can include the address, check-in time and a link to a video showing them the location of the key safe and how it operates.

Next level leverage

The first few systems of cleaning, laundry and maintenance have freed you up to manage your business from anywhere in the world. You are no longer geographically tied to the property. But you still need to organise these on a daily basis, as well as dealing with all the guest queries that your automated messages and emails don't satisfy. There is a way to go before this business is running like clockwork without you.

Employing a virtual assistant

At this point you can think about employing a virtual assistant (VA) to help with the admin work and free up your time. VAs are people who work remotely from anywhere in the world but can answer emails and even phone calls as if they work in your business. With training, they can mop up all the day-to-day jobs you are still doing *in* the business.

VAs can be found on a variety of different platforms such as Upwork (www.upwork.com), Fiverr (www.fiverr.com) and PeoplePerHour (www.peopleperhour.com). They can range in hourly rate depending on where in the world you source them.

Many channel managers offer different levels of access, so you can give login details to a VA with the confidence that they only have permissions within the system to see and do what you want them to do.

Be under no illusion, it can be a long and frustrating process to find the right candidate for your business and it's unlikely that the first person you select will work. It will also be a steep learning curve for you to train them in the exact way you run your business and how you want them to perform.

A VA will be the face of your business and the person your guests speak to, so they need to have an approach that is in line with your values and what is expected in hospitality. There's no point in offering an amazing property if your VA is going to be rude or slow to respond to your guests.

You will need to spend time developing a training manual that gives your VA all the information they will need to effectively communicate with guests. For example, if a guest asks if your property has a coffee machine or hypoallergenic pillows, the VA needs to know in order to respond.

Employing a local manager

If and when your business starts to scale, you might want to directly employ a local manager. Someone on the ground in the area is definitely a better option than someone 500 miles away. The VA system is not perfect and there are instances when someone will need to go to the property, such as if a key safe is jammed or in some other emergency. This is certainly a more expensive option, but it will mean total freedom for you.

Summary

The realities of an SA business hit hard when you get up and running. Without active planning and effort to tame the beast, it can and will take over your life. Trust me, I was there. The excitement you felt at the start when your first booking dropped into your inbox can turn into resentment of guests for their constant and incessant demands. Why don't they read those damn emails?

You can miss out on thousands of pounds of income because you don't have the time to effectively manage your rates, reducing them in panic when you realise you have a gap coming up next week. Weekends and holidays can be ruined by spending all your time cleaning or answering emails and phone calls. Yes, you could be saving money, but you're losing out on so much precious time, which is our most valuable commodity of all.

I hope this chapter has shown you the harsh realities of what your SA business could be, but also how you can push through them by sharpening the axe. You can design and build a thriving business that can be managed remotely from anywhere in the world, taking up only a few hours of your time per week.

Without a sharp axe, you will be stuck at one or two properties. You'll feel overworked and underpaid, like you're drowning and struggling to get your head above the water. By systemising everything laid out in this chapter, you will be able to scale your business quickly and efficiently.

Yes, these systems and processes cost money to implement. Cleaners, linen hire, repairs, channels managers, rate pricing software, text messaging services, VAs and managers are not free. But they're not a cost either. They are all investments that pay for themselves many times over by giving you freedom: both geographically and in time.

Your ability to generate income will no longer be related to the number of hours you work. These systems also give you the capacity to grow your portfolio of SA properties, knowing you have an army of well-oiled systems that you can plug new properties into with minimal effort and cost.

Each time you grow, you'll find yourself doing less work but still earning more money. I'm not saying it'll be easy, but you aren't working *in* the business anymore so you can spend all your time working *on* the business, focusing on new systems to implement or improving current ones.

The next Fundamental 'Protection' will equip you with the street-smarts you need to develop to protect your amazing business from any undesirable people who want to come and stay.

6
Fundamental 5: Protection

Similar to the last chapter, you might fall into one of two camps regarding Fundamental 5: Protection. Is the fear of your place being trashed by partiers one of the biggest things holding you back in getting started? You've heard the horror stories and worry about how you would cope if anything like that ever happened to you. Or maybe you're blissfully unaware of the issues that can occur in SA properties, assuming that all guests who book your place will be good people just looking to have a nice break away, who will treat your property with the respect it deserves. The reality is that there are a *lot* of bad guests out there. You should be concerned. The horror stories are not fairy tales – they are very much real life, and they can happen to you if you're not careful.

Types of bad guests

While the party horror stories get the headlines, these are just one set of guests that you need to protect your place from. Unfortunately for SA operators there is an underworld of unscrupulous and generally unpleasant guests who actively target SA operators. This is in part because they feel they can act with impunity against naïve hosts, but also because of the lack of consequences for their actions and the slim chance of them getting caught before they check out.

Partiers

The alpha of bad guests and the biggest threat to your SA business, these guests cause havoc in all manner of ways. First off is the obvious, they come and have a huge party, leaving a trail of mess and destruction in your property.

They give no care or respect to your place, and you can expect to find rubbish everywhere, evidence of smoking, broken items ranging from glassware to furniture, drug paraphernalia, huge numbers of empty bottles... the list goes on. It's a horribly discouraging sight to walk into and can make you feel either sick to your stomach or filled with rage.

The consequences of having a party in your place are costly. Firstly, you'll have to replace everything that the guests have broken. That's likely to be several glasses or cups, any carpets with cigarette burns in them, broken furniture such as dining chairs, blood-stained linen (fights are common at these events) and any stolen items they may have taken.

On top of that you have a serious cleaning bill coming your way. A standard clean on a two-bedroom apartment can take two hours. Expect that to at least double as bags and bags of empty bottles are collected up and carried out and the floor is mopped at least half a dozen times before it isn't sticky anymore. Even just moving the furniture back to where it's supposed to be takes time. Getting rid of the smell of smoke can also be a costly and tricky exercise (more advice will be given later in the chapter).

There are also more indirect costs of partiers using your place. Your reputation with your neighbours has taken a serious hit and will be hard to rebuild. Most SA operators know and fear the dangers of party bookings, but every homeowner or tenant worries about an Airbnb popping up next door with parties every weekend.

As soon as this happens once, your neighbours will automatically panic that it will be a regular occurrence. They may have given you the benefit of the doubt until now, but as soon as there is a party next door, expect them to turn frosty towards you. You can't blame them either.

Having your neighbours onside is important in SA. They can be your eyes and ears and can alert you to any issues that your guests are causing. You should make sure they know you are on *their* side and that you won't tolerate any form of parties or disruption to their home life.

Prostitutes

These types of guests might not get the headlines compared to partiers, but they are just as insidious and dangerous for your business. Like many industries, it appears that prostitution has moved into the twenty-first century. Gone are the days of people being picked up on street corners. Now they travel around the country (or the world) and advertise their services on escort websites, changing their location each time they move. They tend to stay for longer periods such as seven days and will be using your property as their place of work. These will mainly be an issue for city centre locations or areas of high population.

The consequences of hosting prostitutes are pretty bad. Again, expect some pretty unhappy cleaners as they have to go in and disinfect everything. They will no doubt find used condoms under the beds and some soiled bed linen and towels. You may actually have some cleaners refuse to clean the property based on how bad it is. Would you want to clean up after this?

You'll also have further reputational damage with your neighbours, who will certainly not be happy to be living next door to a pop-up brothel. Again, who can blame them? A steady stream of 'clients' arriving at the property all day and night for over a week is certain to be noticed and cause frustration.

Guests with stolen cards

If you take payments yourself from guests' credit or debit cards, you are at risk of being given stolen or fraudulent card details. Taking payments directly from guests, as discussed in Chapter 3, gives much more flexibility than OTAs charging them on your behalf, but with this added flexibility comes risk. The risk is that you charge a guest's card for the full amount of stay and any additional charges such as late check outs and any damage deposit (there is likely to be damage from these guests). You'll feel pretty happy that at least you got reimbursed for the damage they caused and, hey, they paid a great nightly rate. Then a few months later you'll get notified by your payment processing company that the details you charged were used fraudulently and the real card owner has disputed all the charges. These will be fully reimbursed to the cardholder – at your expense. The guest will have disappeared into the sunset, never to be heard from again. They probably also used a fake name and address, so you have no chance of tracking them down.

If you use OTAs to process your payments, they cover the risk of this happening, which is why they charge for the convenience of their system.

Policy breakers

The three types of bad guests mentioned above definitely cause they biggest cost in terms of financial loss and reputational damage. They are also arguably the easiest to spot – certainly by your cleaners at check out. But there are a few other types of unpleasant guests who you will meet much more frequently and who cause much less – but not insignificant – damage to your business.

Policy breakers can appear in a variety of different situations. They bring pets to a no-pets property; they book a cheaper rate for two people but bring six; they ignore check-in and check-out times. They are out to get whatever they can get – and at your expense.

These are extremely frustrating bookings to deal with as they end up costing you money and time. For example, if a guest brings a dog to your no-pets property, you will have much higher cleaning costs getting rid of all the hair and smells from the property before the next guests arrive. Bookings for two people who show up with six will cost you extra in linen costs. People who ignore your check-in and check-out times will cost you time and stress.

Remember from the last chapter that you need your business to run like clockwork, so if your check-out time is 11am, you will have cleaners at the door at 11.01am ready to get to work. Them being denied access for an hour because the guests are still in bed will cost you money and put the whole team under strain.

The most frustrating thing about these bad guests is that they will generally deny your claims or plead ignorance, for example saying, 'Those dog hairs were there when we arrived' or, 'I never knew check-out was 11am, it's normally 12pm in hotels.'

Refund seekers

These are a particularly nasty set of guests who probably know before they even arrive at your place that they will be seeking some form of refund. Now let me be clear, if a guest genuinely has a bad experience or your place is deficient or not as described, guests *are* entitled to compensation. As I mentioned in Chapter 4, it is good practice to offer compensation before it is requested in circumstances where you have fallen short of delivering a great experience.

However, there are plenty of guests who will request refunds as a standard part of their trip. This is particularly common on Airbnb. Remember that Airbnb holds the booking income until a day after the guest checks in. In my experience, Airbnb will prioritise their own and guest's interests before those of hosts.

If a guest raises any form of complaint to Airbnb, they will usually act to enforce a refund to them. The guest does need to provide some evidence of this where appropriate, but I have seen cases where photos are provided mentioning 'lots of dust' but none is visible, with Airbnb still acting in favour of the guest. In reality, it often seems to be the case that the guest can complain about anything, and Airbnb will favour them. Beds too uncomfortable, area too noisy, property too hot or too cold, unable to work because wi-fi is down… all of these complaints are almost impossible to dispute with evidence, so the guest will get a refund at your expense.

The problem is that many guests have figured this out and now consistently game the system for their own benefit – at your cost.

Review blackmailers

Along similar lines, there are certain guests who will blackmail hosts for refunds, saying that if they don't get a refund, they will leave the property negative reviews. If the standard refund seekers are annoying, the review blackmailers are downright abhorrent. Often, they will wait until after their stay to send you their list of complaints, which is super frustrating because then you have no chance of rectifying them. It's almost like they planned it this way. They'll explain that their stay was disappointing, and they feel that they're entitled to some form of compensation. They'll go on to imply that if this is not forthcoming, they'll have no option but to tell the world in their review just how bad your place was.

Luckily for us, the OTAs do have policies in place to deal with this blackmail. It's reassuring but also shows just how commonplace it is. If you can provide evidence of the blackmail, any negative review will be removed.

How to spot bad guests

You're now well versed on the types of bad guests that will try to book your property. Make no mistake, you will encounter all of these at some point. If you are naïve and too trusting, it will happen sooner and more frequently.

You need to get streetwise, to develop a 'Spidey sense' for these bad guests so you can stop them before they get near your property. It's part intuition, which is built up with experience, but part based on subtle red flags that each of these groups wave via their booking and subsequent communication with you.

On Airbnb you will be able to see guests' past reviews and build up a picture of what other hosts have experienced with them. Unfortunately, there is a bit of a tradition with Airbnb hosts to always leave a five-star review for guests and tell them this in anticipation of a five-star review in return. This obviously ruins the reliability of the review system, and I would always recommend leaving genuine reviews based on your experience. It saves other hosts money and time, and you would certainly be appreciative if you declined an enquiry based on the honest, detailed review given by the previous unlucky person to host this guest.

Of course, guests with a history of negative reviews can simply deactivate that account and set up a new one with no reviews. This is the risk hosts take in accepting bookings from guests with no reviews, especially if the account has been created very recently (this can be seen on a guest's profile when an enquiry is sent).

On Booking.com there is a facility whereby you can 'report guest misconduct' if a guest has caused issues during their stay.[6] When a booking comes in via Booking.com, hosts can click on the guest's name in the extranet and bring up information from their past bookings. Among other things, it shows information like how often they cancel bookings, what average review scores they give and whether they have been reported for misconduct issues.

Identifying partiers

The biggest red flag for partiers is a local address. This isn't visible on Airbnb but is on Booking.com and Expedia bookings. If you see a booking come in with a home address less than ten miles from your property, you have to ask yourself: why does this person need my property?

---

6   Booking.com, 'Reporting guest misconduct', https://partner. booking.com/en-gb/help/first-steps/first-reservations/reporting- guest-misconduct, accessed 16 January 2023

Bookings from international visitors are far less likely to cause any problems. These guests will be travelling for tourism or business and are not just interested in having a knees-up.

If the booking is for all adults, another red flag is waving at you. Chances are that these four locals will know a lot more locals who would love somewhere cool to party – somewhere they don't have to worry too much about looking after because it isn't any of their places.

All large groups of adults should be treated with some level of caution. The reality is that it's extremely unlikely that a family booking is going to party and wreck your place. Likewise, if you have six international visitors, as before, it's unlikely they are here to cause problems.

It goes without saying that weekend bookings are much more dangerous than weekday ones because of the potential for parties. Often those that pay the highest rates should be investigated the most.

Let me explain: you might think a good way to stop parties in your place is to raise the price substantially at the weekend to stop any undesirables booking it. Surely it will be too expensive for them so they'll be priced out and only the more well-off, respectable guests will be able to afford it? Right?

Wrong. If you raise your prices too high, you actually become unaffordable to the nice families paying for the whole place out of one pocket. But the stag party of ten who plan to squeeze into your place all weekend? Well they're splitting the bill ten ways, so it's a bargain for them all.

Detecting prostitutes

One of the biggest red flags for prostitutes is their length of stay. They do tend to stay a lot longer than other guests. The bookings tend to be one or two women, sometimes accompanied by a male. They frequently ask for properties with a view to the street and/or an intercom where they can let people into the main door from the property, claiming they have friends or family visiting.

How to protect yourself and your property

I hope that you don't see this chapter as a downer after the highs of the previous ones. SA is an amazing business to be in and the potential to make great money is real. This chapter is more of a reality check, in case you thought that it would all be easy. It won't.

At the same time, this is not meant to put you off getting started for fear of encountering these guests.

They do exist and they will try to book your place. But you *can* stop them, most of the time. There will be a constant game of cat and mouse going on as you suspect and vet guests in a variety of different ways. Your 'Spidey sense' is a muscle that must be trained and developed.

You will learn to trust your gut and ask the right questions, spotting patterns and similarities among bookings and cancelling them the minute you uncover their true intentions. This will feel uncomfortable at first. After all, we've spoken in Chapter 4 about how important it is to deliver exceptional customer service. Now I'm telling you to quiz guests and cancel bookings, but the alternative is much worse. This is the price of doing business in the SA industry.

Below are some steps and techniques you can employ to keep your property and reputation safe from these bad guests.

Check them out at check in

Meeting guests when they arrive is a great way to give you peace of mind (or not) about who will be staying in your property. You can finally put a face to the name on your booking. Seeing people in the flesh gives you much more information than you can get via email or on the phone.

If you're checking in a group of 'four adults' and five carloads show up, you can have a good idea that a party is planned for your place.

If a booking of two adults and two children arrive and you discover it's two eighteen year olds and two seventeen year olds (this actually happened to me), you can refuse entry.

When you're asking the group of six guys checking in what they have planned for their stay and all they want to know is where the best bars and strip clubs are, it's likely you have a stag party.

Likewise, when two attractive but quiet women arrive with a heavy-set guy who does all the talking and can't give you one single thing they are planning on doing during their stay, it's likely you have a pop-up brothel.

Minimum length of stay

Enforcing a longer minimum stay is the most effective way to stop party bookings. Not many people can hack a three-day bender. The vast majority of party bookings will be for one night, closely followed by two nights. This is a blunt instrument as there are, of course, many genuine guests who only want to stay for one night. There are other bad guests, such as prostitutes, that will stay for longer than three nights.

But, to stop the party bookings, this is the most efficient way. The added extra is that your business will be more profitable as a result of not relying on much shorter stays with huge changeover costs.

Minimum age limits

Minimum age limits are another blunt but effective tool in stopping parties. The highest likelihood of parties will always be from younger people. Anyone over thirty reading this will concur! Yes, you can still get some pretty rowdy stag and hen parties for over thirties, but the regular and consistent stream of party bookings will be people in their early twenties and under. We set our minimum check-in age to twenty-five.

To stress again, there are plenty of people under twenty-five who will be perfect guests and there are people over twenty-five who will be horrible. Your minimum age limit does not have to be set in stone and strictly enforced; you can make exceptions wherever you want. But by having it in place, you give yourself the option to cancel any booking you're uncomfortable with.

House rules

This is your property, and you get to decide what goes on in it. Create a list of house rules that all guests need to adhere to. These should be strict enough to stop any antisocial behaviour but relaxed enough to not affect the stay of any 'normal' guests. Good things to add here are quiet hours, check-in and check-out times and strictly no parties. You want to have everything in writing and displayed in the property so that if the worst happens you can cite a breach of your house rules and remove guests immediately.

You may also decide to include charges for any breaches of the house rules. These can be for things like lost keys, additional cleaning, evidence of smoking and unauthorised late check out. Again, these are only aimed at those guests engaged in antisocial behaviour. Please do not become a host that gives a huge list of tasks to do, while also charging guests a cleaning fee. It's not fair and people hate it.

Security deposits

A security deposit is a token deterrent against bad guests causing damage to your place. It can also be a way of discouraging bad guests to book in the first place if they know they'll have to pay it.

Why do I call it a token deterrent? Well, the simple fact is that bad guests can cause a lot more damage than a £250 security deposit will cover. A broken bed, a ruined carpet from spilled drinks and cigarette burns, or any other damage caused by a party can easily exceed £250. Security deposits should be taken before check in and the guests clearly informed that it will be returned after check out, once your house-keeping team have got in and confirmed everything is in order. You should also clearly communicate on what grounds the security deposit will be retained.

Try to get the deposit from the lead booker. That way you can expect them to police the rest of the group as it's their money being held and their profile that will be tarnished.

It does have to be open and fair. It's not there as a punishment as much as reimbursement for your costs. You can't find evidence of smoking and retain a full £250 security deposit, but you should include your own time in any calculations of how much to retain.

Vetting procedure

If you're not planning on meeting and greeting guests, a strong vetting procedure is absolutely crucial. Even if you are meeting guests on arrival, employing this vetting procedure will save you time and hassle by getting any dodgy bookings that slipped through your policies cancelled *before* they arrive.

There are several steps to vet bookings you're suspicious of. Your hope is that any concerns you have are completely dispelled: this is the best-case scenario. Worst case is that your concerns get worse the more you find out. In these cases, you will probably know enough to get that booking cancelled.

If you notice a booking come in with a local address and you're worried it might be a party, these are the steps to take. It goes without saying that no key safe codes should be given out until you are satisfied there won't be any issue.

Step 1: Research the guest online

Look up the guest's name and phone number on Google, Facebook, etc and view their social media profiles. Look at their WhatsApp profile picture. Do you notice anything suspicious? Are they smoking a joint? Do they look younger than your minimum check-in age?

Step 2: Phone the guest

Phone the guest and enquire as to the reason of their stay. You're using your great customer service to build that rapport, but you also want to figure out why they've booked your place. Ask them nice questions such as what they have planned and whether they need any help. You can also ask them straight up why they booked your place when they live so close by. It's important you speak to the guest on the phone – email or text are not sufficient. Anyone can craft a perfectly worded email to throw you off the scent, but phoning them will catch them off-guard.

Step 3: Explain that parties are not allowed

Outline that, as per your house rules, parties and social gatherings in the property are not allowed and that if a complaint is made by a neighbour then unfortunately, they will be removed from the property immediately. You can explain that this has happened in the past and is unpleasant for everyone, especially because the police will be involved. Clearly and assertively tell the guests that if they are planning to have any form of party, your property isn't the right place for them and if that's their plan then they can cancel now and find somewhere more suitable.

Step 4: Get written confirmation

Get written confirmation from the guest that they agree to comply with your house rules. This is the perfect opportunity for the guest to realise this whole party is not worth it and request a cancellation.

Step 5: Obtain photographic ID

Obtain photographic ID – passports or driving licences only – for everyone staying in the property. Tell the guests this list will be passed on to your 'security team'. If they are called out and anyone other than these people are in the property, everyone will have to leave. This also gives you the opportunity to make sure everyone is over your minimum check-in age.

Step 6: Take your security deposit

Explain you need to take a security deposit of £250. The card used must belong to the lead guest. If they want another guest to provide the card, they must get email confirmation from the guest that they accept responsibility for any additional charges set out in your house rules. Only accept a card from someone staying in the property who you have ID for.

Step 7: Be suspicious until proven otherwise

The approach is to be suspicious by default until convinced otherwise. If in any doubt, politely inform the guest that you are not comfortable with their reservation, and they will not be staying. If guests are unhappy to comply with any requests, it's best to let them cancel for free. You've dodged a bullet. All correspondence should also be done via email to the guest so you can provide evidence against any chargebacks.

CCTV

If you plan to install any CCTV at your property, the only place you can do it is outside the front door. For guests' privacy, you should not have CCTV anywhere inside the property. Even having it on the outside should be clearly signposted.

You can tell guests about how the CCTV is there for their safety in your initial communications. This is, of course, true, but it's also true that if they try to sneak twenty people in at night, you'll be able to see it happening. Or if there is a steady stream of men coming into the property, you'll be able to ask why this is happening.

There are lots of different types of CCTV available. You want one that you can view live from your phone. You can get products that alert you when there is movement at the door, so you'll be able to view the interesting timestamps in the morning instead of scrolling through hours of footage to see if people were coming and going through the night.

Make sure that the power cable is not accessible to guests, or they will simply switch it off so you can't see what's happening. They aren't stupid remember!

Noise monitors

While you can't have CCTV in your property you *can* install noise monitors. These devices don't record anything being said in the property, they just measure the sound levels and alert you if they get too loud. Again, this should be communicated to guests during your vetting procedure.

3DS payment links or chip and pin

If you're processing payments directly from a guest's card before check in, the best way to protect against a chargeback is to send them a payment link so the guest enters their card details and makes the payment themselves. This is secure because the cardholder will have to enter a one-time passcode to prove it's them making the transaction.

Taking payment at check in using a chip and pin terminal is the other way. By ensuring the guest enters their pin and doesn't use contactless, the transaction cannot be charged back.

What to do when it all goes wrong

You've followed all the advice in this chapter but a bad guest still manages to slip through the net – what do you do?

Get lots of evidence

If you're unlucky enough to have your place used for a party, it's crucial that your housekeeper gets photos or videos of the mess and everything that has been damaged. They obviously need to do this before they start cleaning. If you are claiming from Airbnb insurance or retaining a portion of a security deposit, you will need this evidence to support your case. Without evidence, the guests can dispute your claim.

Be strong

Refuse entry to anyone you want – this is *your* property. When we become so reliant on OTAs like Airbnb for our business, it can be easy to fall into the trap of giving them too much respect. If you have strong suspicions about a booking and tell Airbnb you don't want to host them, the chances are Airbnb will give you no support and tell you the booking has to happen.

Airbnb can penalise hosts who cancel bookings because it gives guests a bad experience on their site. You cannot become or remain a Superhost if you cancel bookings. It can feel like you're stuck between a rock and a hard place: on one hand you're worried about the booking and your place being damaged and on the other hand you're worried about being penalised by Airbnb. My advice is to be strong and remember that this is *your* property. *You* are the one who will have to deal with the complaints, damage and unhappy housekeepers.

When refund seekers and review blackmailers come to you looking for money back for false complaints, again be strong. It's horrible to get a bad review, but if you have done nothing wrong and the complaints are false, you should not bow to these demands. It's worth mentioning again that if a guest genuinely has a bad experience, you should of course offer some form of refund. While it is likely to stop a bad review, this is also just the right thing to do.

Just ignore those who are out to get what they can at your expense. Even if they do leave a review, you can report it to the OTAs along with evidence of their blackmail. The OTA will then remove that bad review. You can also reply publicly to all reviews so you can explain to anyone who might be reading it the actual circumstances that led to the negativity.

People understand that things go wrong, and one or two bad reviews will not ruin your property's ability to generate bookings, especially if you are working hard and delivering exceptional experiences for everyone else who stays with you. Your average review score will remain high.

Mark guest misconduct

If a booking comes into your place and causes one of the issues mentioned above, it's good practice to mark them so future hosts can get a heads up.

On Airbnb that comes in the form of leaving the guest a negative but truthful review, which will be visible to all future hosts the guest enquires about.

On Booking.com it means going into their booking and reporting guest misconduct. This not only means that Booking.com know this is a bad guest, but it also lets future hosts see this before the guest checks in. Unfortunately, as previously mentioned, Booking.com don't do enquiries so these guests will be able to book your place. But you will be able to take additional steps to ensure they know what is and isn't acceptable and, if necessary, tell them they won't be staying.

How to get rid of smoke smells

Guests smoking in your property can cause a lot of damage, but one of the worst things is the smell lingering in your soft furnishings. This can be anxiety inducing, especially if you have new guests checking in on the same day as the bad guests leave. It's the same if you walk into a strong smell of dog, fish or Indian food.

The best and fastest way to get rid of these smells is to use an ozone generator. This machine completely eliminates all odours in your property, including pets, food and smoke, in a few hours. To see the exact product I recommend, follow the link at the back of the book.

Summary

The harsh reality of SA is that there are some horrible bookings out there and they're coming your way. Partiers, prostitutes, stolen credit cards, policy breakers, review blackmailers... the list goes on. It's up to you to get streetwise and put policies in place to weed them out and prevent them getting into your property.

The policies you choose will stop a lot of them, but some will still slip through the net, if you let them. Your 'Spidey sense' muscle will need to be trained to spot those guests who will cost you time, money and stress.

You need to get tough because, let's face it, you're on your own when it comes to the OTAs. They don't care who's booking your place as long as they're booking through their system. Trying to get these bad bookings cancelled will be a struggle but remember that as the host *you* get to decide who stays and who doesn't.

Bad bookings will cause you reputational damage with your neighbours and cleaners. They'll cost you money in replacing or repairing items and additional cleaning time. They'll also cause you so much stress: before the guests check in, during their stay and even after they've gone.

Remember, this is your property, and you need to protect your investment. It's set up for those perfect guests who you want to have a great time. Hosting a few bad bookings will seriously affect your ability to deliver for those guests.

7
Final Thoughts

By now you're fully equipped with the knowledge to start an SA business that will from day one be better than 99% of the properties in your area. You're starting with the knowledge and expertise that I have built up over fifteen years. The time, stress and money that you'll save are vast and your progress will be rapid if you implement all the recommendations in this book. You'll have the hottest property in town and a business that's generating significant and consistent income right away, giving you financial and time freedom to live life on your terms.

From Fundamental 1, you now know how to research and choose the right property, what exactly you'll need to put into it and who's going to stay in it. This will ensure you get the highest return from your investment.

Fundamental 2 showed you exactly how to get bookings and where to go for them and it introduced you to the benefits of channel managers. This will bring you maximum exposure online, so you are not reliant on just one source of bookings.

Fundamental 3 gave clarity on just what to expect from guests, including the common things they ask about, as well as discussing the mindset shift that is needed when starting a hospitality business. This will ensure you get those five-star reviews and can continue to charge the highest rates.

From Fundamental 4 you have unlocked the time freedom this business can deliver through systems. You now have clarity on what you need to leverage and when, freeing up more and more of your time as you grow and build a business that runs like clockwork while you're asleep or lying on a beach.

Finally, Fundamental 5 gave you the street-smarts you need to protect yourself and your property from bad guests. Stopping those bookings at source will save you money and stress, keeping your amazing property filled with the right kind of guests.

Values and mindset

I want to finish by talking about some of the values that I hope you've noticed weaved throughout this book, which should be a guiding light when an unexpected situation or decision arises. These values enabled me to get to where I am today and have resulted in the successes I have achieved so far.

Grit

Starting a new venture is exciting and terrifying for everyone. There's all that initial energy about the future you're creating for yourself and your family, but after a while the fear and anxiety can kick in. Like in any business, you will suffer setbacks and things that don't go your way.

It can be hard to keep motivated once the initial shine wears off and you're faced with the reality that it's all up to you to make this work. No one's going to come and hand you a pay cheque every month, you need to go out and get it. This is where grit comes in. Like Rocky says, 'It ain't about how hard you hit, it's about how hard you can get hit and keep moving forward.'[7]

Rolling with the punches and learning from mistakes is how we all become successful. I've developed grit through accepting the wrong bookings, taking on the wrong properties, employing the wrong people, Covid… the list goes on. Each time, it feels like a punch in the face, but each time you get a little bit more resilient, the punches hurt a little less and you get better at dodging them.

Innovation

Being willing to try new things or change current practices is key to success. One example is how you decorate your property. Lots of people like to play it safe and follow what everyone else is doing in terms of colour and design. The problem is that every property ends up looking the same and you get lost in the crowd.

Push the boundaries. Use bold colours, quirky designs and neon signs. Market a houseboat, a treehouse or even somewhere specifically aimed at stag and hen parties.

---

7   S Stallone, 'It ain't about how hard you hit', *Rocky Balboa* (MGM Studios, 2006), www.youtube.com/watch?v=kyQrl7AWeXg, accessed 24 January 2023

For me, innovation has always been important, and I knew I wanted to stand out among the crowd. From the second property I renovated, I added chalkboard walls and painted doors pink and yellow. This grew to buying and renovating a five-bedroom HMO into seven en suite serviced rooms because we were getting so many enquiries for solo travellers who couldn't afford a whole apartment. Finally, I embraced video content – TikTok in particular – to grow our reach and develop my personal brand. I'm always thinking about ways to do things differently.

Constant self-improvement

If you follow the steps in this book, you will have a fantastic SA business generating significant income and tons of happy guests. But why should it stop there? Do you even know what you'd be capable of if you pushed yourself to get 1% better every day?

Like the systems, there are always ways to improve how things are done – efficiencies that can be made and extra revenue that can be secured. But it's not just the functional aspects of the business, it's you too – your mindset, goals and outlook. By constantly working on yourself you will reach a potential you never knew you had.

You could end up writing a book, or get paid to speak on stage, or build a worldwide SA brand. Who knows what doors will open when you keep pushing yourself forward every day.

Growth mindset

A growth mindset is when you believe that no ability or skill is fixed, that no one is 'good' or 'bad' at anything and that anyone can improve at anything with enough practice and focus.

You must have some form of growth mindset if you're hoping to start an SA business that you have no experience in. But maybe there are aspects in the book that you're not so keen on because you don't think you'd be any good at them. Perhaps that's designing a colour scheme for a property, phoning guests you've never met, learning how to run Facebook Ads or talking to the camera to make video content.

There will be things you know you need to do but feel scared about because you've never done them before, and they make you feel uncomfortable. By getting comfortable being uncomfortable, you can take massive steps forward in your life and success.

I struggled with talking on camera, even though I knew it was something I needed to do. If you look back on my early videos on YouTube, you'll see how nervous I was. But I kept forcing myself to do it and now I have a pretty big following across YouTube, TikTok, podcasts, etc. I knew if I kept doing it, I would get better.

Goal setting

Having a clear vision of what exactly it is you want to achieve is going to help you get it. Are you wanting to set up this SA to replace your income from work so you can quit? If so, when do you want that to happen by? How many properties do you need?

Once you know your end goal, you can formulate all the smaller goals that you need to achieve for that to happen. If you write these steps down every day, they will become fixed in your mind like a roadmap, and you'll know exactly what you need to do to move yourself closer to your goal.

Another great thing about having goals is that it gives you opportunities to celebrate when you reach them. Realising you've achieved a goal you've been working hard towards is an amazing feeling, which helps to motivate you to keep pushing.

My early goal was to replace my income from work. It then developed into having complete time freedom and being able to work remotely from anywhere in the world. More recently it's been writing this book you're reading and the coaching and courses I'm working on next.

Leverage

As you've read throughout the book, you simply cannot run this business without the help of others.

Whether that's your cleaners or the OTAs, you will to some degree have to leverage tasks out. The question you should ask yourself every day is: 'What/who can I get to do this for me?'

With websites like Upwork and Fiverr, you can find people from around the world who specialise in the jobs and tasks you need to get done, from VAs to website developers to social media agencies. If there's something you know you need to do for your business but aren't doing it because you don't have the time or expertise, find someone else to do it.

Leveraging other people's time and expertise enables you to grow your business and reach at an unbelievable rate. Instead of having twenty-four hours in a day, you can have an infinite amount by using people and programmes to work on your behalf.

Coaching

Without doubt, one of the things that has contributed the most to my growth has been working with a coach. Like I mentioned earlier, starting a new business is hard, scary, uncomfortable and, at times, lonely.

No one else knows the specific reality of what you're going through. Friends and family in jobs might not have that entrepreneurial spirit you have and will wonder why you're putting yourself through it. A coach offers support like no other. They are deter-mined to see you succeed and will give you support as well as accountability to make sure you keep push-ing towards those goals you've set.

Before I had a coach, I was still driven and determined. The business was growing, but I kept floundering at times and procrastinating over big decisions. I felt imposter syndrome, like I didn't know what I was doing, and I lacked confidence in myself.

I first started working with my coach during spring 2020, right at the start of the pandemic. Travel restric-tions had just decimated our future bookings, but I knew the pandemic would not last forever. In those first few months, when I felt I had no control over what was happening, I decided that I would work on things I *could* control. I wanted to come out of the pandemic in a much stronger position than I entered into it.

That's exactly what happened. Coaching has improved my mindset significantly. I've done things I'd only ever dreamt of like speaking on stage, writing books and growing a YouTube channel. The boost that coaching has given me has been incredible.

My business has grown at a faster rate than ever before. I'm more confident and effective and my life has never been better. I can directly attribute so much of where I am today to the coach I work with.

This is why I've decided to start coaching myself to help those just starting out who were in my position with all those same questions and concerns. It's the reason for this book. The clients I work with through my courses, workshops and coaching programmes get clarity and confidence and are able to accelerate their progress by leveraging my experience and expertise.

Further support

Here are some suggestions of things to do to nurture that entrepreneurial mindset and help you succeed in your SA business. They work for me – choose the ones you think will help you.

Work with me

I'd love to help you on your journey so you can reach your goals faster. You can find all the other ways to work with me by clicking this link (www.stan.store/airbnb-coach) or scanning the QR code.

Keep educating yourself

You've read this book, which is a fantastic start. I hope you feel equipped and ready to take on the SA industry. But, like I keep saying, this is a business, so you need to think like a businessperson.

There are so many incredible business and self-development books out there to help sharpen your mindset and give you the tools you need to succeed. I remember the first business book I ever read and the fire it gave me to get going. I've never lost that excitement. I've read dozens of incredible books from some of the most successful people and leaders on the planet.

I've compiled a list of my favourites and the ones that have had the greatest impact on my life. I actually prefer audiobooks as I can listen to them when I'm out running or in the car (another great example of leverage). You can see the list of all my recommendations (both paperback and audiobook) here: www.amazon. co.uk/shop/davecordnercentralbelfastapartments.

Mindset recommendations

By practising gratitude, Wim Hof breathing and the power of cold water, you too can become more mindful, focused and content.

Gratitude

Practising gratitude every day has been one of the most significant things I've ever added into my life.

We're all striving for things and that can lead us to feel unfulfilled and discontented with where we are now.

We can easily overlook or underappreciate all the amazing things we have in our life or the small wins we get each day because we're so focused on the future and where we want to get to. Practising gratitude makes us stop and recognise how far we've already come and helps to keep us present in the moment or the day.

I have two books that I thoroughly recommend to help you practise gratitude. I use them every day and have seen an amazing lift in my mood and outlook as a result. These are both by Dominik Spenst: *The 6-Minute Success Journal* and *The 6-Minute Diary*.[8]

Wim Hof

I practice Wim Hof breathing on a daily basis as part of my morning routine. I'm not going to cite any health benefits here – you can research those for yourself – but I find the practice helps with stress and lifts my overall mood.

It's like meditation for me, and I use the 'breath hold' to refocus my thoughts to be positive and optimistic, silently reciting affirmations that are helpful to me. If

---

8   D Spenst, The 6-Minute Success Journal (UrBestSelf, 2020) and The 6-Minute Diary (UrBestSelf, 2019), https://urbestself.co, accessed 10 February 2023

you search Wim Hof on YouTube, you'll find free videos where he guides you through the technique.[9]

Cold water

The health benefits of getting into cold water are well documented. Again, I'm not going to spell them out here, but I will talk about the mood benefits that I've experienced since starting the practice.

As well as getting into the Irish sea at least once a week, I have a cold shower every morning. It never gets any easier. Every time I stand on the shore or start to turn the temperature dial on the shower to cold, I get the same anxiety. Every time, I think I don't want to do this, but each time I force myself to. It's a small act but a significant win for the day and a great way to build that muscle of getting comfortable feeling uncomfortable.

It's also a great way to clear your head and destress. Getting into the sea in winter will 100% take your mind off anything else that's worrying you! The cold is such a shock to your body that you have to focus fully on your breathing. Afterwards, it feels great because you've pushed yourself to do something you knew was going to be tough.

---

9   Guided Wim Hof Method Breathing, www.youtube.com/watch?v=tybOi4hjZFQ, accessed 10 February 2023

Acknowledgements

I'd like to thank all the people who have helped me on my journey so far, starting with my parents, Stephen and Jane. You have both always supported and encouraged me in whatever I've done. The decision to buy your first SA started this whole journey. It gave me the opportunity to learn the best practices and what's required in this business. You loaned me the money to buy my first place and everything I've built has been thanks to you.

My wife, Katie, who put up with so much at the start of our relationship while I was trying to get the business off the ground: interrupted date nights, helping me clean the properties and putting up with mountains of dirty linen in our house. I promised you it wouldn't always be like that, and you trusted me. No matter how crazy and frequent my ideas are, you always listen and encourage me. You got me through the worst days of my life during those first few weeks of Covid. You push me when I'm doubting myself and lift me up when I'm feeling down.

My two boys, Jack and Tom. Everything I've built is because of you. I wanted a life where I was present for all your milestones. I didn't want to miss a second of you growing up. I wanted to be able to play all day or take you to school or go on holiday whenever we wanted. I also want you to be proud of me and what I've done, and that spurs me on every day. You can do anything you want in life, and I will always support you both.

Brian Muldoon, my coach. When I look back to where I was in June 2020 when we first started working together and see how much things have changed, it's incredible! Every little idea I've had has come to pass thanks to your belief and accountability. You've helped get this plane off the runway. Being a business owner can be a lonely and scary place and you continue to be an amazing friend and companion on my journey.

Chris and Mary Selwood who helped me switch from business owner to teacher by co-hosting my first workshop on the five fundamentals. You're an incredible and inspirational team and two of the nicest, most giving people I've ever met.

Cheryl McCook and the whole Central Belfast Apartments team, thank you for all your hard work *in* the business that allows me the headspace to work *on* the business. Without you, none of this would exist. Your dedication to serve our guests and deliver exceptional experiences is incredible. You're all rockstars!

My friend, Craig Thompson, and the Swimrisers: Anthony Keiran, Ciaran May, Mark O'Neill, Eddie McCrea, Marty McNicholl and Marty McDonnell. What an amazing set of inspirational business owners who lift each other up and spur each other on.

Matthew McGeady and the team at Right Now Social for helping me become 'that guy off TikTok'.

Daniel Priestley, for being a guiding light on my journey. *Entrepreneur Revolution* was the first ever business book I read, and it lit a fire inside me.[10] Your article at the start of Covid about how to spend a bounce back loan had a profound impact on me and helped us come out of the pandemic in a much stronger position.[11] The KPI accelerator was one of the best investments I've ever made and has culminated in this book. I will forever be a huge fan.

Thank you to all the beta readers of the early drafts of this book: Katie Jackson, Anthony Keiran, Kevin Kerr, Mark Simpson and Martin Malseed. All your feedback was so useful and much appreciated.

---

10 Priestley, D, *Entrepreneur Revolution: How to develop your entrepreneurial mindset and start a business that works* (Capstone, 2013)

11 Priestley, D, 'How to spend £50K (EG: A Bounceback Loan)', LinkedIn (4 May 2020), www.linkedin.com/pulse/how-spend-50k-daniel-priestley, accessed 18 January 2023

The Author

Dave Cordner is the founder of Central Belfast Apartments, the biggest serviced accommodation management company in Northern Ireland, managing a property portfolio of more than sixty properties worth over £10 million.

Dave has been involved in SA for fifteen years and has built up considerable expertise in this time, hosting tens of thousands of guests and working with brands such as BBC, Netflix and BT.

In 2022 Central Belfast Apartments won Best Serviced Apartment Operator at the Serviced Apartment

Awards and Northern Ireland's Leading Serviced Apartments at the World Travel Awards.

Dave has led Central Belfast Apartments to number one on Tripadvisor and in 2020 and 2022 the company won a Tripadvisor Travellers' Choice Award, putting them in the top 10% of hotels worldwide.

He and Central Belfast Apartments have been featured regularly in the media, from tourism bodies like Tourism Ireland and Visit Belfast to newspapers and digital publications.

Dave shares his considerable expertise on a daily basis through his various social platforms. He also offers coaching programmes for those who want to accelerate their SA businesses.

🌐 www.davecordner.com

▶️ www.youtube.com/c/DaveCordnerCentral BelfastApartments

🔗 www.linkedin.com/in/dave-cordner

📷 www.instagram.com/_airbnbcoach

♪ www.tiktok.com/@airbnbcoach

www.ingramcontent.com/pod-product-compliance
Ingram Content Group UK Ltd.
Pitfield, Milton Keynes, MK11 3LW, UK
UKHW021047070725
6753UKWH00057B/1642